Horatius Bonar

Lyra Consolationis

Hymns for the Day of Sorrow and Weariness

Horatius Bonar

Lyra Consolationis
Hymns for the Day of Sorrow and Weariness

ISBN/EAN: 9783337779375

Printed in Europe, USA, Canada, Australia, Japan

Cover: Foto ©Lupo / pixelio.de

More available books at **www.hansebooks.com**

LYRA CONSOLATIONIS

OR

HYMNS FOR THE DAY OF SORROW & WEARINESS

EDITED BY

HORATIUS BONAR, D.D.

NEW YORK
ROBERT CARTER & BROTHERS
530 BROADWAY

1866

CONTENTS.

CONTENTS.

CONTENTS.

CONTENTS.

CONTENTS.

Page

SWEET CUP OF SORROW.

SWEET cup of sorrow,
  I would drink thee !
Cup of unearthly wine,
As thy lip touches mine,
  I would bethink me,—
" Christ, my joy and hope,
  Once drained a bitterer cup,
Let me then drink thee up !"

Dear cup of sorrow,
  I would own thee !
And speak thy praises true,
As only those can do
  Who have known thee.

Sweet and bitter joined
Medicine of soul and mind,
Health in thee let me find !

Though thou art bitter,
    Love is in thee ;
Pledge of the brighter wine,
Let my pale lips touch thine,
    For within thee
Are the blessings seven ;
O cup, O wine of heaven,
At the high banquet given !

DIVINE SYMPATHY.

Jesus, my sorrow lies too deep
   For human ministry;
It knows not how to tell itself
   To any but to Thee.

Thou dost remember still, amid
   The glories of God's throne,
The sorrows of mortality,
   For they were once thine own.

Yes : for, as if thou wouldst be God,
   Even in thy misery,
There's been no sorrow but thine own,
   Untouched by sympathy.

Jesus, my fainting spirit brings
   Its fearfulness to Thee ;
Thine eye, at least, can penetrate
   The clouded mystery.

And is it not, O Lord, enough
    This holy sympathy?
There is no sorrow e'er so deep
    But I may bring to Thee.

It is enough, my precious Lord,
    Thy tender sympathy!
My every sin and sorrow can
    Devolve itself on Thee.

As God, thou graspedst e'en the whole
    Of human misery;—
Thine own alone lay desolate,
    That Thou mightst pitied be.

Thy risen life but whets Thee more
    For kindly sympathy;
Thy love unhindered rests upon
    Each bruised branch in Thee.

Jesus! thou hast availed to probe
    My deepest malady;
It freely flows—more freely finds
    The gracious remedy.

LADY POWERSCOURT.

BEYOND THE SKIES

WE seek a rest beyond the skies,
    In everlasting day ;
Thro' floods and flames the passage lies,
    But Jesus guards the way.
The swelling flood and raging flame
    Hear and obey his word ;
Then let us triumph in his name,
    Our Saviour is the Lord.

NEWTON.

HOPE'S RAINBOW.

Though the heart that sorrow chideth
   Sink in anguish and in care;
Yet, if patience still abideth,
   Hope shall paint her rainbow there.
Faith's bright lamp her light shall borrow
   From religion's blessed ray,
And from many a coming morrow
   Charm the clouds of grief away.

Wherefore should we sigh and languish,
   When our cares so soon shall cease,
And the heart that sows in anguish
   Shall hereafter reap in peace?
This is not a scene of pleasure,
   These are not the shores of bliss;
We shall gain a brighter treasure,
   Find a dearer land than this.

Anon.

GOD IS LOVE.

Who fathoms the Eternal Thought?
   Who talks of scheme and plan?
The Lord is God! he needeth not
   The poor device of man.

I walk with bare hushed feet the ground
   Ye tread with boldness shod;
I dare not fix with mete and bound
   The love and power of God.

Ye praise his justice; even such
   His pitying love I deem;
Ye seek a king; I fain would touch
   The robe that hath no seam.

Ye see the curse which overbroods
   A world of pain and loss;
I hear our Lord's beatitudes
   And prayer upon the cross.

More than your schoolmen teach, within
    Myself, alas, I know ;
Too dark ye cannot paint the sin,
    Too small the merit show.

I bow my forehead to the dust,
    I veil my eyes for shame,
And urge, in trembling self-distrust,
    A prayer without a claim.

I see the wrong that round me lies,
    I feel the guilt within ;
I hear, with groans and travail-cries,
    The world confess its sin :

Yet in the maddening maze of things,
    And tossed by storm and flood,
To one fixed star my spirit clings :
    I know that God is good !

Not mine to look when cherubim
    And seraphs may not see,
But nothing can be good in him
    Which evil is in me.

The wrong that pains my soul below
  I dare not throne above ;
I know not of his hate—I know
  His goodness and his love.

I dimly guess from blessings known,
  Of greater out of sight,
And, with the chastened Psalmist, own
  His judgments too are right.

I long for household voices gone,
  For vanished smiles I long,
But God hath led my dear ones on,
  And He can do no wrong.

I know not what the future hath
  Of marvel or surprise,
Assured alone that life and death
  His mercy underlies.

And if my heart and flesh are weak
  To bear an untried pain,
The bruised reed He will not break,
  But strengthen and sustain.

No offering of my own I have,
   Nor works my faith to prove;
I can but give the gifts he gave,
   And plead his love for love.

And so beside the silent sea
   I wait the muffled oar;
No harm from him can come to me
   On ocean or on shore.

I know not where his islands lift
   Their fronted balms in air;
I only know I cannot drift
   Beyond his love and care.

O brothers! if my faith is vain,
   If hopes like these betray,
Pray for me, that my feet may gain
   The sure and safer way.

And Thou, O Lord! by whom are seen
   Thy creatures as they be,
Forgive me if too close I lean
   My human heart on Thee!

                  WHITTIER.

LABOUR AND REST.

"Two hands upon the breast, and labour is past."
Russian Proverb.

"Two hands upon the breast,
    And labour's done :
Two pale feet crossed in rest,
    The race is run :
Two eyes with coin-weights shut,
    And all tears cease :
Two lips where grief is mute,
    And wrath at peace."
So pray we oftentimes, mourning our lot ;
God in his kindness answereth not.

"Two hands to work addrest
    Aye for his praise :
Two feet that never rest,
    Walking his ways :

Two eyes that look above,
    Still through all tears :
Two lips that breathe but love,
    Nevermore fears."
So cry we afterwards, low at our knees,
Pardon those erring prayers ! Father, hear
    these.

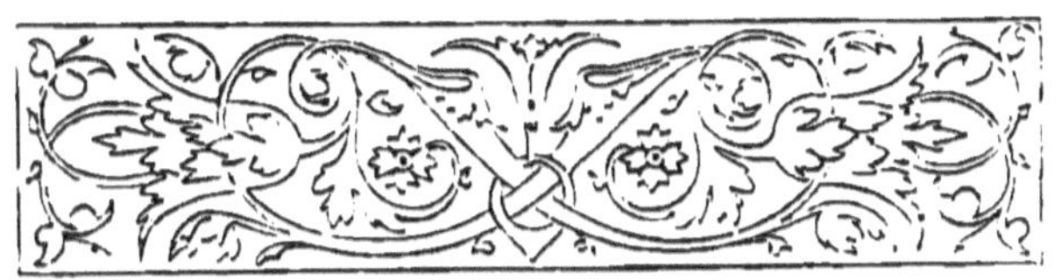

THE THREE WEEPERS.

Sorrow weeps !—

    And drowns its bitterness in tears ;
    My child of sorrow,
    Weep out the fulness of thy passionate grief,
    And drown in tears
    The bitterness of lonely years.
    God gives the rain and sunshine mild,
    And both are best, my child !

Joy weeps !—

    And overflows its banks with tears ;
    My child of joy,
    Weep out the gladness of thy pent-up heart,
    And let thy glistening eyes
    Run over in their ecstasies ;
    Life needeth joy ; but from on high
    Descends what cannot die !

Love weeps !—
> And feeds its silent life with tears ;
> My child of love,
> Pour out the riches of thy yearning heart,
> And, like the air of even,
> Give and take back the dew of heaven ;
> And let that longing heart of thine
> Feed upon love divine !

H. BONAR.

MY GOD, MY ALL.

My soul doth pant towards Thee,
   My God, source of eternal life,
Flesh fights with me :
   O end the strife,
And part us, that I may
                    Unclay
My wearied spirit, and take
   My flesh to thy eternal spring,
Where, for his sake
   Who is my King,
I may wash all my tears away,
                    That day !
Thou Conqueror of death,
   Glorious triumpher o'er the grave,
Whose holy breath
   Was spent to save
Lost mankind, make me to be styled
                    Thy child !

And take me when I die,
    And go unto my dust ; my soul
Above the sky
    With saints enrol
That in thy arms for ever I
            May lie !

                    JEREMY TAYLOR.

THY DARLING IS NOT DEAD.

Look up, look up and weep not so ;
  Thy darling is not dead ;
His sinless soul is cleaving now
  Yon sky's empurpled bed :
His spirit drinks new life and light
  Mid bowers of endless bloom :
It is but perishable stuff
  That moulders in the tomb.
Then hush, O hush the swelling sigh
  And dry the idle tear,
Look out upon yon glorious heaven
  And joy that he is there.
Already hath he gained the goal
  And tasted of the bliss,
The peace that God's pervading love
  Prepares for souls like his.
Then calm thy sorrow-stricken heart,
  And smile away despair ;
Think of the home thy child hath won
  And joy that he is there.

When summer evening's golden hues
   Are burning in the sky
And odorous gales from balmy bowers
   Are breathing softly by;
When earth is bright with sunset's beams
   And flowers are blushing near;
And grief, all chastened and subdued,
   Is gathering to a tear:
How sweet 'twill be, at such an hour,
   And mid a scene so fair,
To lift thy streaming eyes to heaven,
   And think that he is there!
And when that final hour arrives,
   The hour that all must brave,
Ere thy full ear of life be reaped,
   And garnered in the grave;
While deeply musing on the fate
   Our prayers may not defer,
What ardent longings after bliss
   Each failing pulse will stir!
How sweet will be the glance to heaven,
   The heaven thou soon mayst share;
The memory of thy buried babe,
   The hope to meet him there!

ALARIC A. WATTS.

MY PSALM.

I MOURN no more my vanished years ;
   Beneath a tender rain,
An April rain of smiles and tears,
   My heart is young again.

The west winds blow, and, singing low
   I hear the glad streams run ;
The windows of my soul I throw
   Wide open to the sun.

No longer forward nor behind
   I look in hope and fear ;
But, grateful, take the good I find,
   The best of now and here.

I plough no more a desert land,
   To harvest weed and tare ;
The manna dropping from God's hand
   Rebukes my painful care.

I break my pilgrim staff, I lay
   Aside the toiling oar ;
The angel sought so far away
   I welcome at my door.

The airs of spring may never play
   Among the ripening corn,
Nor freshness of the flowers of May
   Blow through the autumn morn ;

Yet shall the blue-eyed gentian look
   Through fringed lids to heaven,
And the pale aster in the brook
   Shall see its image given ;

The woods shall wear their robes of praise,
   The south wind softly sigh,
And sweet, calm days in golden haze
   Melt down the amber sky.

Not less shall manly deed and word
   Rebuke an age of wrong ;
The graven flowers that wreathe the sword
   Make not the blade less strong.

But smiting hands shall learn to heal,
  To build as to destroy;
Nor less my heart for others feel
  That I the more enjoy.

All as God wills, who wisely heeds
  To give or to withhold,
And knoweth more of all my needs
  Than all my prayers have told!

Enough that blessings undeserved
  Have marked my erring track—
That whereso'er my feet have swerved.
  His chastening turned me back—

That more and more a Providence
  Of love is understood,
Making the springs of time and sense
  Sweet with eternal good—

That death seems but a covered way
  Which opens into light,
Wherein no blinded child can stray
  Beyond the Father's sight—

That care and trial seem at last,
　　Through Memory's sunset air,
Like mountain-ranges overpast,
　　In purple distance fair—

That all the jarring notes of life
　　Seem blending in a psalm,
And all the angles of its strife
　　Slow rounding into calm.

And so the shadows fall apart,
　　And so the west winds play;
And all the windows of my heart
　　I open to the day.

WHITTIER.

THE CHRISTIAN DEAD.

THEY dread no storm that lowers,
    No perished joy bewail ;
They pluck no thorn-clad flowers,
    Nor drink of streams that fail :
There is no tear-drop in their eye,
    Nor change upon their brow ;
The placid bosom heaves no sigh,
    Though all earth's idols bow.

Who are so greatly blessed ?
    From whom hath sorrow fled?
Who find such deep unbroken rest,
    While all things toil ?—The dead !
The holy dead !—Why weep ye so
    Above their sable bier ?
Thrice blessed ! they have done with woe,—
    The living claim the tear.

We dream, but they awake;
   Dark visions mar our rest;
Mid thorns and snares our way we take,
   And yet we mourn the blest.
For those who throng the eternal throne,
   Lost are the tears we shed:
They are the living, they alone,
   Whom thus we call the dead.

SIGOURNEY.

THE GLORY TO BE REVEALED.

THE time will come when every change shall cease.
This quick revolving wheel shall rest in peace ;
No summer then shall glow, nor winter freeze ;
Nothing shall be to come, and nothing past,
But an eternal now shall ever last.
Though time shall be no more, yet space shall give
A nobler theatre to love and live.
Then all the lying vanities of life,
The sordid source of envy, hate, and strife,
Ignoble as they are, shall then appear
Beneath the searching beam of truth severe.
Then souls, from sense refined, shall see the fraud
That led them from the living way of God.
Blest is the pile that marks the hallowed dust,
There, at the resurrection of the just,
When the last trumpet, with earth-shaking sound,
Shall wake her sleepers from their couch profound ;
How will the beatific sight display
All heavenly beauty in these climes of day !

PETRARCH.

SHORT SORROW, LONG JOY.

AFTER long storms and tempests' sad assay,
   Which hardly I endured heretofore,
In dread of death, and dangerous dismay,
   With which my silly bark was tossed sore,
   I do at length descry the happy shore
In which I hope, ere long, for to arrive;
   Fair soil it seems from far, and fraught with store
Of all that dear and dainty is alive.
Most happy he that can at last achieve
   The joyous safety of so sweet a rest;
Whose least delight sufficeth to deprive
   Remembrance of all pains which him oppressed.
All pains are nothing in respect of this;
All sorrows short that gain eternal bliss.

EDMUND SPENSER.

COME, LORD JESUS!

GREAT joy to me it were to join the throng,
    That thy celestial throne, O Lord, surround,
    Where perfect peace and pardon shall be found,—
Peace for good doings, pardon for the wrong;
Great joy to hear the vault of heaven prolong
    That everlasting trumpet's mighty sound,
    That shall to each award their final bound,—
Wailing to these, to those the blissful song.

GUITTONE D'AREZZO, A.D. 1527.

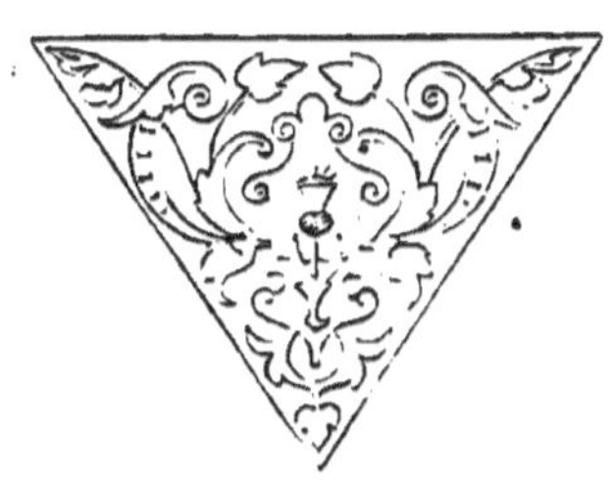

THY DAUGHTER IS DEAD.

I KNOW the *child* is fled ;
A lovely *maiden* comes to me in dreams,
Yet the same splendour in her blue eye beams,
While sunny hair ripples in wavy gleams
    Around the fair young head ;
I know she moves, the central star to light
A pastor's home : long be that hearthstone bright.

    Beyond the shadowy pale
I stretch my hand, and paint her destiny
With rainbow hue ; a flowery life-road see,
Then trembling cry—My God it rests with Thee.
    Alas, a low deep wail
From breaking hearts ; I know the fair is fled ;
" Death found strange beauty ;" swift his arrow sped.

Our Father, 'tis thy hand !
The stricken feel it, yet 'tis hard to say,
Thy will be done—No parent near, to lay
In those cold arms a darling's form of clay,
And with the spirit stand
Neath the bright portals of eternal day,
Till sister spirits beckoned her away.

It could not be, O God !
It could not be ! then fold them tenderly
In thy Almighty arms ; soothe lovingly
Each bleeding heart, and fill with heaven and
Thee ;
So shall they kiss the rod.
The soul her shining wing shall lift from dust,
And sing—"Although He slay me, I will trust."

O. E. REYNOLD.

THANK THE LORD FOR SORROW.

THANK the Lord for every sorrow,
  Thank Him for the keenest smart;
Pleasures trouble's pathway follow;
  Anguish lifts from earth the heart.

The summer's hot, oppressive ray,
  Ripens but the luscious fruits;
On the rough briar's thorny spray
  Oft the fairest flower shoots.

The stars most brightly shine on high
  In the deepest, darkest night;
'Tis only through a cloudy sky
  Bends the rainbow's glorious light.

Take, then, sorrow as a treasure,
  Thankfully from God's kind hand;
For th' unfailing cup of pleasure
  Waits thee in the better land.

FROM THE GERMAN.

THE GOD OF ABRAHAM.

THE God of Abraham praise !
Who reigns enthroned above :
Ancient of everlasting days,
    And God of love ;
Jehovah, Great I Am !
By earth and heaven confessed ;
I bow and bless the sacred name,
    For ever bless'd.

The God of Abraham praise !
At whose supreme command
From earth I rise—and seek the joys
    At his right hand ;
I all on earth forsake,
Its wisdom, fame, and power,
And him my only portion make,
    My shield and tower.

The God of Abraham praise !
Whose all-sufficient grace
Shall guide me all my happy days,
In all his ways :
He calls a worm his friend !
He calls himself my God !
And He shall save me to the end,
Through Jesus' blood.

He by himself hath sworn,
I on his oath depend,
I shall, on eagles' wings up-borne,
To heaven ascend :
I shall behold his face,
I shall his power adore,
And sing the wonders of his grace
For evermore.

Though nature's strength decay,
And earth and hell withstand,
To Canaan's bounds I urge my way,
At his command :
The watery deep I pass,
With Jesus in my view ;

And through the howling wilderness
　　My way pursue.

The goodly land I see,
　With peace and plenty bless'd;
A land of sacred liberty,
　　And endless rest :
There milk and honey flow,
　And oil and wine abound ;
And trees of life for ever grow,
　　With mercy crown'd.

There dwells the Lord our King,
　The Lord our Righteousness,
Triumphant o'er the world and sin,
　　The Prince of Peace !
On Zion's sacred height
　His kingdom still maintains ;
And glorious, with his saints in light
　　For ever reigns.

He keeps his own secure,
　He guards them by his side,
Arrays in garments white and pure,
　　His spotless bride ;

With streams of sacred bliss,
With groves of living joys,
With all the fruits of paradise,
He still supplies.

Before the Three in One,
They all exulting stand,
And tell the wonders He hath done,
Through all their land.
The listening spheres attend,
And swell the growing fame,
And sing in songs which never end,
The wondrous Name.

OLIVER.

OUR GOLDEN DAY.

HAVE we not now a golden daye?
   The Lorde prolonge the same!
That in his fear henceforth we may
   Practise our lives to frame;

And so be thankful to our God
   For these his gifts of grace;
That He may still behold our days
   With his most loving face.

That all our wordes and deedes henceforth
   May lerne so to accord,
That we, with harts unfained, may
   Still live and laude the Lorde.

Increase the number of thy falde;
   Thy mercie, Lord, displaie;
Prolonge, amonge thy simple sheepe,
   This happy golden daie.

Come, haste thy kingdome, mighty God,
  Come, Jesus Christ, we praie,
That all our foes may learne and know
  We have a golden daie.

Which to continue longe,
  To God let us all pray;
Whose glorious name be lauded still
  For this our golden daie.

JOHN PHILLIP, 1570.

CLINGING.

CLING to the Mighty One,
   Cling in thy grief :
Cling to the Holy One,
   He gives relief.
Cling to the Gracious One,
   Cling in thy pain :
Cling to the Faithful One,
   He will sustain.

Cling to the Living One,
   Cling in thy woe :
Cling to the Loving One,
   Through all below :
Cling to the Pardoning. One,
   He speaketh peace :
Cling to·the Healing One,
   Anguish will cease.

Cling to the Bleeding One,
   Cling to his side :
Cling to the Rising One,
   In Him abide :
Cling to the Coming One,
   Hope shall arise :
Cling to the Reigning One,
   Joy lights thine eyes.

ANON.

THE UNCHANGEABLE.

WHAT though time on earth were over?
  Not on time our hopes depend;
Lo, beyond it, we discover
    Life that never knows an end.
    'Mid the woes that life attend,
  · Still for rest we turn to Thee:
  God, a father and a friend,
    Changeless, in his Son we see.

Father still in all our need,
  Father still in weal or woe:
Father even of the dead,
    When into the grave we go.
    Change may toss us to and fro,
    Changeless He in whom we trust:
  Even our dust his care shall know,
    When our bodies turn to dust.

Then let days and years be fleeting,
 Swiftly pass our joys and woes;
'Mid the changes we are meeting,
 God, our God, no changes knows.
Ours be then a life that shows
 That, conducted by his hand,
We shall enter at its close
 Our beloved father-land.

FROM THE DUTCH.

OUR ALL.

ART thou weak, afflicted soul?
I am strong to make thee whole.
Art thou sick, and hast no cure?
I am thy Physician sure.
Art thou fainting on thy road?
I am near to bear thy load.
Art thou hungry, thirsty, poor?
I am rich to bless thy store.
Art thou much with grief opprest?
I am come to give thee rest.
Art thou weary of thy sin?
I am peace to thee within.
I am ready at thy side,
At thy right and left to guide.
I am life, and love, and peace,—
I am joy which ne'er shall cease.

ANON.

RETURNING CLOUDS.

THE clouds are returning after the rain ;
  All the long morning they steadily sweep
From the blue northwest, o'er the upper main,
  In a peaceful flight to the eastern deep.

With sails that the cool wind fills or furls,
  And shadows that darken the billowy grass,
Freighted with amber or piled with pearls,
  Fleets of fair argosies rise and pass.

The earth smiles back to the smiling throng
  From greening pasture and blooming field,
For the earth, that hath sickened with thirst so
    long,
  Has been touched by the hand of the rain,
    and healed.

The old man sits 'neath the tall elm trees,
   And watches the pageant with dreamy eyes,
While his white locks stir to the same cool breeze
   That scatters the silver along the skies.

The old man's eyelids are wet with tears—
   Tears of sweet pleasure and sweeter pain—
For his thoughts are driving back over the years
   In beautiful clouds after life's long rain.

Sorrows that drowned all the springs of his life,
   Trials that crushed him with pitiless beat,
Storms of temptation and tempests of strife,
   Float o'er his memory tranquil and sweet.

And the old man's spirit, made soft and bright
   By the long, long rain that hath bent him low,
Sees a vision of angels on wings of white,
   In the drooping clouds as they come and go.

AMERICAN.

PASS OVER TO THY REST.

FROM this bleak hill of storms,
To yon warm sunny heights,
Where love for ever shines,
      Pass over to thy rest,
      The rest of God !

From hunger and from thirst,
From toil and weariness,
From shadows and from dreams,
      Pass over to thy rest,
      The rest of God !

From tides, and winds, and waves,
From shipwrecks of the deep,
From parted anchors here,
      Pass over to thy rest,
      The rest of God !

From weakness and from pain,
From trembling and from strife,
From watchings and from fears,
>> Pass over to thy rest,
>> The rest of God!

From vanity and lies,
From mockery and snares,
From disappointed hopes,
>> Pass over to thy rest,
>> The rest of God!

From falsehoods of the age,
From broken ties and hearts,
From suns gone down at noon,
>> Pass over to thy rest,
>> The rest of God!

From unrealities,
From hollow scenes of change,
From ache and emptiness,
>> Pass over to thy rest,
>> The rest of God!

From this unanchored world,
Whose morrow none can tell,
From all things restless here,
Pass over to thy rest,
The rest of God !

H. BONAR.

READY TO DEPART.

I'M going to leave all my sadness,
    I'm going to change earth for heaven :
There, there, all is peace, all is gladness,
    There pureness and glory are given.
        Come quickly then, Jesus !   Amen !

Friends, weep not in sorrow of spirit,
    But joy that my time here is o'er ;
I go the good part to inherit,
    Where sorrow and sin are no more.
        Come quickly then, Jesus !   Amen !

The shadows of evening are fleeing,
    Morn breaks from the city of light ;
This moment day starts into being,
    Eternity bursts on my sight.
        Come quickly then, Jesus !   Amen !

The first-born redeemed from all trouble,
  (The Lamb that was slain, in the throng),
Their ardour in praising redouble ;—
  Breaks not on the ear the new song ?
    Come quickly then, Jesus ! Amen !

I'm going to tell their glad story,
  To share in their transports of praise ;
I'm going in garments of glory,
  My voice to unite with their lays.
    Come quickly then, Jesus ! Amen !

Ye fetters corrupted, then leave me ;
  Thou body of sin, droop and die ;
Pains of earth, cease ye ever to grieve me ;
  From you 'tis for ever I fly.
    Come quickly then, Jesus ! Amen !
                 Malan.

CROSS AND CROWN.

Jesus, our head, once crowned with thorns,
  Is crowned with glory now;
Heaven's royal diadem adorns
  The mighty victor's brow.

Delight of all who dwell above,
  The joy of saints below;
To us still manifest thy love,
  That we its depths may know.

To us thy cross, with all its shame,
  With all its grace, be given!
Though earth disowns thy lowly name,
  All worship it in heaven.

Who suffer with Thee, Lord, below,
  Will reign with Thee above;
Then let it be our joy to know
  This way of peace and love.

To us thy cross is life and health,
  Though shame and death to Thee,
Our present glory, joy, and wealth,
  Our everlasting stay.

ANON.

THE REFINER.

God's furnace doth in Zion stand,
    But Zion's God sits by ;
As the refiner views his gold
    With an observant eye.
God's thoughts are high, his love is wise,
    His wounds a cure intend ;
And though He doth not always smile,
    He loves unto the end.

Thy love is constant to its line,
    Though clouds oft come between ;
O could my faith but pierce these clouds,
    It might be always seen.
But I am weak, and forced to cry,
    Take up my soul to Thee ;
Then, as Thou ever art the same,
    So shall I ever be.

Then shall I ever, ever sing,
  While Thou dost ever shine:
I have thine own dear pledge for this,
  Lord, Thou art ever mine.

Mason, 1683.

I AM WITH THEE

On mountains and in valleys,
  Where'er we go is God ;
The cottage and the palace
  Alike are his abode.

In sinking and in soaring,
  Thought finds Him ever near,—
Where angels are adoring,
  Where fiends believe and fear.

With watchful eye abiding
  Upon us with delight :
Our souls, in Him confiding,
  He keeps both day and night.

Above me and beside me.
  My God is ever near,—
To watch, protect, and guide me,
  Whatever ills appear.

Though other friends may fail me
In sorrow's dark abode,—
Though death itself assail me,
I'm ever safe with God.

FROM THE DUTCH.

LIGHT OUT OF DARKNESS.

God moves in a mysterious way
   His wonders to perform;
He plants his footsteps in the sea,
   And rides upon the storm.

Deep in unfathomable mines
   Of never-failing skill,
He treasures up his bright designs,
   And works his sov'reign will.

Ye fearful saints, fresh courage take,
   The clouds ye so much dread
Are big with mercy, and shall break
   In blessings on your head.

Judge not the Lord by feeble sense,
   But trust Him for his grace:
Behind a frowning providence
   He hides a smiling face.

His purposes will ripen fast,
 Unfolding every hour;
The bud may have a bitter taste,
 But sweet will be the flower.

Blind unbelief is sure to err,
 And scan his work in vain :
God is his own interpreter,
 And He will make it plain.

NEWTON.

IT IS WELL.

Beloved, " it is well !"
  God's ways are always right ;
And love is o'er them all,
  Though far above our sight.
Beloved, " it is well !"
  Though deep and sore the smart,
He wounds, who knows to bind
  And heal the broken heart.

Beloved, " it is well !"
  Though sorrow clouds our way,
'Twill make the joy more dear
  That ushers in the day.
Beloved, " it is well !"
  The path that Jesus trod,
Though rough and dark it be,
  Leads home to heaven and God.

Anon.

ALL IN GOD.

O LOVED, but not enough ;—though dearer far
Than self, and its most loved enjoyments are !
None duly loves Thee, but who, nobly free
From sensual objects, finds his all in Thee.

Glorious, Almighty, First, and without end !
When wilt Thou melt the mountains and descend ?
When wilt Thou shoot abroad thy conquering rays,
And teach these atoms Thou hast made thy praise !

GUION.

DIVINE COMPANIONSHIP.

WHEN quiet in my house I sit,
  Thy book be my companion still,
My joy thy sayings to repeat,—
  Talk o'er the records of thy will,
And search the oracles divine,
Till every heart-felt word be mine.

O may the gracious words divine
  Subject of all my converse be ;
So will the Lord his follower join,
  And walk and talk himself with me :
So shall my heart his presence prove,
And burn with everlasting love.

Oft as I lay me down to rest,
  O may the reconciling word
Sweetly compose my weary breast !
  While on the bosom of my Lord
I sink in blissful dreams away,—
And visions of eternal day.

Rising to sing my Saviour's praise,
   Thee may I publish all day long;
And let thy precious word of grace
   Flow from my heart and fill my tongue!
Fill all my life with purest love,
And join me to the church above.

WESLEY.

WITHIN SIGHT OF CANAAN.

O Israel, who is like to thee?
A people saved, and called to be
　　Peculiar to the Lord !
Thy shield ! He guards thee from the foe :
Thy sword ! He fights thy battles too,
　　Himself thy great reward.

Thy toils have almost reached a close,
Thou soon art destined to repose
　　Within the promised land :
Its rising hills ev'n now are seen
Enrich'd with everlasting green,
　　Where thou so soon shalt stand.

Sweet hope ! it makes the coward brave,
It makes a freeman of the slave,
　　And bids the sluggard rise ;
It lifts a worm of earth on high,
It gives him wings, and bids him fly
　　To everlasting joys.　　　　　Anon.

THE DEATH OF MOSES.

Sweet was the journey to the sky
    The holy prophet tried ;
" Climb up the mount," said God, " and die ;"
    The prophet climbed, and died.

Softly, with fainting head, he lay
    Upon his Maker's breast ;
His Maker soothed his soul away,
    And laid his flesh to rest.

In God's own arms he left the breath
    That God's own Spirit gave ;
His was the noblest road to death,
    And his the sweetest grave.

Watts.

IT WILL SOON BE WELL.

My span of life will soon be done,
   The passing moments say ;
As lengthening shadows o'er the plain
   Proclaim the close of day.
Soon will the toilsome strife be o'er
   Of weariness and care ;
And life's dull vanities no more
   This anxious heart ensnare.

Courage, my soul ! thy bitter cross,
   In every trial here,
Shall bear thee to thy heaven above,
   But shall not enter there.
Courage, my soul ! on God rely,
   Deliverance soon shall come ;
A thousand ways thy Saviour has
   To bring his people home.

Mrs. Cowper,
Aunt of the Poet.

IT IS THE LORD.

It is the Lord—enthroned in light,
   Whose claims are all divine ;
Who has an undisputed right
   To govern me and mine.
It is the Lord—should I distrust
   Or contradict his will,
Who cannot do but what is just,
   And must be righteous still ?

It is the Lord—who gives me all,—
   My wealth, my friends, my ease ;
And of his bounties may recall
   Whatever part He please.
It is the Lord—who can sustain
   Beneath the heaviest load :
From whom assistance I obtain,
   To tread the thorny road.

It is the Lord—whose matchless skill
  Can from afflictions raise
Blessings, eternity to fill
  With ever-growing praise.
It is the Lord—my covenant God—
  Thrice blessed be his name,
Whose gracious promise, seal'd with blood,
  Must ever be the same.

GREENE.

THE PARTING AND THE MEETING.

WHEN friend from friend is parting,
   And in each speaking eye
The silent tears are starting,
   To tell what words deny,—
How could we bear the heavy load
   Of such heart-agony,
Could we not cast it all, our God,
   Our gracious God, on Thee ;
And feel that Thou kind watch wilt keep
   When we are far away,—
That Thou wilt soothe us when we weep,
   And hear us when we pray?

Yet oft these hearts will whisper—
   That better 'twould betide,
If we were near the friends we love,
   And watching by their side.
But sure thou'lt love them dearer, Lord,
   For trusting Thee alone,

And sure Thou wilt draw nearer, Lord,
  The farther we are gone.
Then why be sad, since 'Thou wilt keep
  Watch o'er them day by day;
Since Thou wilt soothe them when they weep,
  And hear us when we pray?

O for that bright and happy land,
  Where, far amid the blest,
The wicked cease from troubling, and
  The weary are at rest!
Where friends are never parted,
  Once met around thy throne;
And none are broken-hearted,
  Since all with Thee are one!
Yet, Oh, till then, watch o'er us keep,
  When far from Thee away,
And soothe us, Lord, oft as we weep,
  And hear us when we pray.

MONSELL.

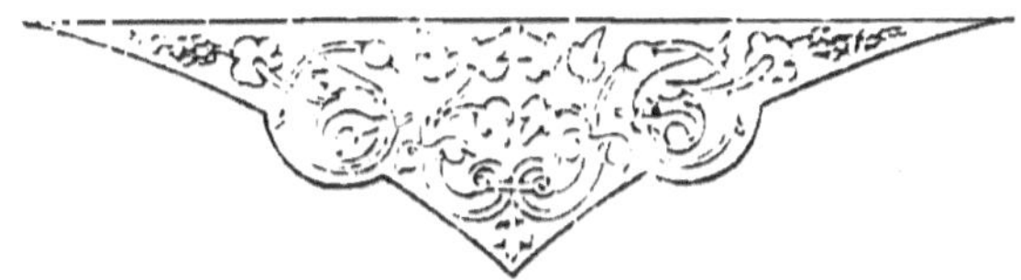

ALL IS WELL.

IF my bark be strong,
  If my anchor sure,
Then let billow upon billow beat ;
  Am I not secure ?
On the dreariest, wildest sea,
What are winds to me ?

Up between the stars
  Spreads night's tranquil blue ;
Not one ruffle, not one wrinkle there
  Blots the changeless hue.
Storms of earth for earth are given ;
But they reach not heaven !

To that heaven I go,
  To that starland bright,
Where the sea is ever smooth and fair,
  And the sky all bright ;
Never heavy, pale, or dull ;—
Starland beautiful !

Therefore am I calm ;
  Peace and love within.
That dear light, that on me gently falls,
  Casts out fear and sin.
As my home above is. so
Am I now below.

H. BONAR.

PRAISE FOR THE HOPE OF GLORY.

I SOJOURN in a vale of tears ;
    Alas, how can I sing !
My harp doth on the willows hang,
    Distuned in every string.
My music is a captive's chains,
    Harsh sounds my ears do fill ;
How shall I sing sweet Zion's song
    On this side Zion's hill ?

Yet lo, I hear a joyful sound,
    " Surely I quickly come ;"
Each word much sweetness doth distil,
    Like a full honey-comb.
And dost Thou come, my dearest Lord ?
    And dost Thou surely come ?
And dost Thou surely quickly come ?
    Methinks I am at home.

Come then, my dearest, dearest Lord,
    My sweetest, surest friend ;

Come, for I loathe these Kedar tents ;
　Thy fiery chariots send.
What have I here ?   My thoughts and joys
　Are all pack'd up and gone ;
My eager soul would follow them
　To thine eternal throne.

What have I in this barren land ?
　My Jesus is not here ;
Mine eyes will ne'er be blest until
　My Jesus doth appear:
My Jesus is gone up to heav'n,
　To get a place for me ;
For 'tis his will that where He is,
　There should his servants be.

Canaan I view from Pisgah's top ;
　Of Canaan's grapes I taste ;
My Lord, who sends unto me here,
　Will send for me at last.
I have a God that changeth not,
　Why should I be perplext ?
My God, that owns me in this world,
　Will own me in the next.

Go fearless, then, my soul, with God,
  Into another room;
Thou, who hast walked with Him here,
  Go see thy God at home.
View death with a believing eye,
  It hath an angel's face;
And this kind angel will prefer
  Thee to an angel's place.

The grave is but a fining pot
  Unto believing eyes:
For there the flesh shall lose its dross,
  And like the sun shall rise.
The world, which I have known too well.
  Hath mock'd me with its lies;
How gladly could I leave behind
  Its vexing vanities?

My dearest friends they dwell above,
  Them will I go to see;
And all my friends in Christ below
  Will soon come after me.
Fear not the trump's earth-rending sound.
  Dread not the day of doom;

For He, that is to be thy judge,
  Thy Saviour is become.

Blest be my God that gives me light,
  Who in the dark did grope ;
Blest be my God, the God of love,
  Who causeth me to hope.
Here's the Word's signet, Comfort's staff,
  And here is Grace's chain ;
By these thy pledges, Lord, I know
  My hopes are not in vain.

J. MASON.

SAVIOUR BE NEAR.

My Saviour, be Thou near me
      Through life's night;
I cry, and Thou wilt hear me,—
      Be my light!
My dim sight aching,
Gently Thou'rt making
Meet for awaking
      Where all is bright!

Oh, through time's swelling ocean
      Be my Guide!
From tempest's wild commotion
      Hide, O hide!
Life's crystal river
Storms ruffle never;
Anchor me ever
      On that calm tide!
          M. L. DUNCAN.

MY PILGRIMAGE.

WHAT is this life ?   A constant scene
Of sighs and tears, of care and pain.
   Moments of sin and months of woe
      Here ebb and flow,
   Till we are summoned hence to go.

And what is man ?   A clod of earth,
A needy mortal from his birth :
   Brought nothing with him when he came,
      But sin and shame,
   And naked leaves this earthly frame.

Evil and few have been my days,
Weary and sad my pilgrim-ways,
   When God shall call his servant home,
      I'll seek the tomb,
   In hope of endless joys to come.

Amen ! Thou sovereign God of love
Grant us thy bliss when we remove ;
That we, redeemed by thy blood,
May find in God
Our everlasting sure abode.

MORAVIAN.

MY REDEEMER LIVETH.

"I KNOW that my Redeemer lives,"
What comfort that sweet sentence gives !
He lives ! He lives ! who once was dead :
He lives, my everlasting Head !
He lives, triumphant from the grave :
He lives, eternally to save.

He lives, all glorious in the sky ;
He lives, exalted there on high ;
He lives, to bless me with his love ;
He lives, to plead my cause above ;
He lives, to upbind and make me whole ;
He lives, to calm my troubled soul.

He lives, to grant me rich supply ;
He lives, to guard me with his eye ;
He lives, my hungry soul to feed ;
He lives, to help in time of need ;
He lives, that He may in me dwell ;
He lives, to crush the powers of hell.

He lives, to silence all my fears;
He lives, to stop and dry my tears;
He lives, my kind, wise, heavenly friend;
He lives, and loves me to the end;
He lives, my Prophet, Priest, and King;
He lives, and while He lives, I'll sing.

He lives, to grant me daily breath;
He lives, and I shall conquer death;
He lives, my mansion to prepare;
He lives, to bring me safely there.
O the sweet joy this sentence gives—
"I know that my Redeemer lives!"

ANON.

THE WAYS OF GOD.

THY ways, O Lord ! with wise design,
   Are framed upon thy throne above ;
And every dark or bending line
   Meets in the centre of thy love.

With feeble light, and half obscure,
   Poor mortals thy arrangements view ;
Not knowing that the least are sure,
   The most mysterious just and true.

My favoured soul shall meekly learn
   To lay her reason at thy throne :
Too weak thy secrets to discern,
   I'll trust Thee for my guide alone.

ANON.

WHO ARE THESE AND WHENCE CAME THEY?

Not from Jerusalem alone,
  To heaven the path ascends;
    As near, as sure, as straight the way
    That leads to the celestial day,
  From farthest realms extends;
Frigid or torrid zone.

What matters how or whence we start?
  One is the crown to all;
    One is the hard but glorious race,
    Whatever be our starting-place;—
  Rings round the earth the call
That says, Arise, depart!

From the balm-breathing, sun-loved isles
  Of the bright southern sea,
    From the dead north's cloud-shadow'd pole,
    We gather to one gladsome goal,—
  One common home in thee,
City of sun and smiles!

The cold rough billow hinders none ;
    Nor helps the calm, fair main ;
        The brown rock of Norwegian gloom,
        The verdure of Tahitian bloom,
    The sands of Mizraim's plain,
Or peaks of Lebanon.

As from the green lands of the vine,
    So from the snow-wastes pale,
        We find the ever-open road
        To the dear city of our God ;
    From Russian steppe, or Burman vale,
Or terraced Palestine.

Not from swift Jordan's sacred stream
    Alone we mount above ;
        Indus or Danube, Thames or Rhone,
        Rivers unsainted and unknown ;—
    From each the home of love
Beckons with heavenly gleam.

Not from gray Olivet alone
    We see the gates of light ;
        From Morven's heath or Jungfrau's snow
        We welcome the descending glow

Of pearl and chrysolite,
And the unsetting sun.

Not from Jerusalem alone
  The Church ascends to God ;
    Strangers of every tongue and clime,
    Pilgrims of every land and time,
  Throng the well-trodden road
That leads up to the throne.

H. Bonar.

RESTING IN HOPE.

Jesus, I cast my soul on Thee,
   Mighty and merciful to save;
Thou wilt to death go down with me,
   And gently lay me in the grave.

This body then shall rest in hope,—
   This body which the worms destroy;
For surely Thou wilt bring me up
   To glorious life and endless joy.

ANON.

THE JOYS OF HEAVEN.

Far from these narrow scenes of night,
  Unbounded glories rise,
And realms of infinite delight,
  Unknown to mortal eyes.
Fair distant land, could mortal eyes
  But half its joys explore,
How would our spirits long to rise,
  And dwell on earth no more !

There pain and sickness never come,
  And grief no more complains;
Health triumphs in immortal bloom,
  And endless pleasure reigns.
No cloud these blissful regions know,
  For ever bright and fair ;
For sin, the source of mortal woe,
  Can never enter there.

There no alternate night is known,
  Nor sun's faint sickly ray,

But glory from the sacred throne
   Spreads everlasting day.
Oh, may the heavenly prospect fire
   Our hearts with ardent love,
Till wings of faith and strong desire
   Bear every thought above.

STEELE.

DEATH OF SAINTS.

Man's life's a sigh, a groan, a cry,
Looks up, and then begins to die;
Death steals upon us while we're green,
Behind us digs a grave unseen.

But oh, how great a mercy's this,
That death's a portal into bliss!
While yet the body's scarce undrest,
The soul is slipt into its rest!

My soul! death swallows up thy fears,
Thy grave-clothes dry off all thy tears;
Why should we fear this parting pain,
Who die that we may live again.

Who walk below in light and love,
Are sure to live with Christ above;
A bosom heaven will afford
To those that live unto the Lord.

O how the resurrection light
Will clarify believers' sight !
How joyful will the saints arise,
And rub the dust from off their eyes !

My soul, my body, I will trust
With Him who numbers every dust;
My Saviour faithfully will keep
His own ; and death is but a sleep.

J. MASON.

SLEEP IN JESUS.

DEATH steals upon us unawares,
  And digs a grave unseen,
Whilst we dispute, are full of cares,
  What may be, what has been.
Shall I be bent on vanity,
  And rottenness to trust,
Till death shall lay his hand on me,
  And crumble me to dust?

What if my sun should set at noon ?
  If death should call to-day,
Canst thou, my soul, go off so soon ?
  Hast thou no scores to pay ?
Behold my sands, how quick they run,
  How near I am my goal ;
Let not my body be undressed,
  Till Thou hast dressed my soul.

That at the trumpet's sound I may
  Spring from my dusty bed,
Rejoicing at the voice that calls,
  Arise, come forth, ye dead.
Lord, give me patience if I lie
  Upon a dying bed,
O let my Saviour, standing by,
  Support my weary head.

Support my weak and tottering faith
  While dismal fears annoy :
My Jesus, be my sweet defence;
  My Jesus, be my joy.
Blest Advocate, do Thou not fail
  At this time to appear,
O let my shaken faith prevail,
  My evidence be clear.

My soul in thy sweet hands I trust,
  Now can I sweetly sleep ;
My body, falling to the dust,
  I leave with Thee to keep.

J. MASON.

DEAD AND RISEN.

A son of man the Son of God
　　Became, and did not scorn ;
On earth, from Mary's virgin womb
　　The holy child was born.

Let me remember all that love,
　　Which in his breast did burn,
When all the wrath of God for sin,
　　Upon his soul did turn ;

When God's own well-beloved Son
　　Went mourning to the grave,
And died accursed for sin, that grace
　　Might dying sinners save.

See from the dead the Prince of Life
　　In glory bright appears ;
No further proof of love I'll seek ;
　　This quiets all my fears.

This bow of light upon the cloud
   Sure token is of grace ;
Where wrath did frown, see mercy smiles,
   From Jesu's loving face.

This sign of love my soul relieves ;
   'Tis ease from all my pain ;
I shall not blush to see Thee, God,
   Because the Lamb was slain.

OLD AUTHOR.

THE JOYS ABOVE.

O WHAT a glorious lot shall then be mine
When God to me shall these bright joys assign !
For there the sovereign good for ever reigns—
No evil yet to come, no present pains ;
No baleful birth of time its inmates fear,
That comes, the burden of the passing year ;
Oh, happy are the blessed souls that sing
Loud hallelujahs in eternal ring !
Thrice happy he, who late, at last shall find
A lot in the celestial climes assigned !
He, led by grace, the auspicious ford explores,
Where cross the plains the wintry torrent roars ;
That troublous tide, where, with incessant strife,
Weak mortals struggle through, and call it life.
One glimpse of glory on the saints bestow'd,
With eager longings fills the courts of God
For deeper views, in that abyss of light ;
While mortals slumber here, content with night.
Though nought we find below the moon can fill
The boundless cravings of the human will.

PETRARCH.

OUR MOTHER'S DEATH.

Silently, over land and sea,
    Came down the winter's night :
Bearing upon its ebon wings
    A mantle purely white.

A spangled robe, as beautiful
    As the Immortals wear ;
And over all the land it spread
    The vesture soft and fair.

Over the frozen river's breast,
    And o'er the town 'twas spread ;
And o'er the monuments and mounds
    Above the quiet dead.

Upon the mountain's lofty head,
    And o'er the fields below,
O softly, softly, every where,
    Came down the gentle snow.

Within our peaceful, sheltered home,
 Where all was bright and warm,
Was one preparing to go forth,
 But not into the storm.

A stranger to our home had come,
 A message there to bring;
Our mother took the scroll, and knew
 The signet of the king.

The bitter, parting hour had come!
 Husband, nor child, nor friend,
Could stand against the stranger's power,
 Nor with his will contend.

We gathered round our mother's bed
 To catch her parting breath;
But one stood *nearer* to her heart;
 We knew his name was Death!

And from our love, and from our grief,
 And from our dwelling warm,
He bore our mother in his arms;
 But not into the storm.

She went unseen, but not alone,
  Dear pilgrim of the earth;
For Jesus took her by the hand,
  And gently bore her forth.

And the sweet word she left for us,
  Shall our life's watchword be :
"As I have followed Jesus' steps,
  Beloved ones, follow me."

We laid her body down to sleep,
  Where all is sweet and still,
Where the last rays of sunlight fall
  Upon the westward hill.

And precious, precious to our hearts
  Shall be that sacred spot,
While by the Lord she loved so well
  It will not be forgot.

Wasted and wan we laid her down;
  Worn out with mortal strife;
But fair and glorious shall she rise
  To glad, eternal life.

Oh ! Heavenly Father, teach us how
    To live and how to die,
That we may with our mother rise
    To immortality.

Augusta Moore (American).

DYING IN THE LORD.

WHEN the glowing pulse of health is beating,
    'Tis *hard* to die ;
When friends surround me with their earnest greeting,
    How hard to die !

Though sickness comes, in waking and in sleeping,
    'Tis *hard* to die !
When true hearts look on me with sighs and weeping,
    How hard to die !

But when the sting of death my Lord is stealing,
    'Tis *sweet* to die !
And when my Saviour smiles, his love revealing,
    How sweet to die !

When all my sins my precious Lord is hiding,
    'Tis *sweet* to die !
And when my soul is to his presence gliding,
    How sweet to die !

Oh, death is *now* but as a blessed river,
 So sweet to die ;
It leads from gifts, up to the glorious Giver ;
 So sweet to die !

There I shall see his beauteous face for ever,
 Oh, sweet to die ;
And leave his presence nevermore, no, never,
 Oh, sweet to die !

D. H. E. (Amurican.)

WEEP NOT FOR ME.

WHEN the spark of life is waning,
    Weep not for me :
When the languid eye is straining,
    Weep not for me :
When the feeble pulse is ceasing,
Start not at its swift decreasing ;
'Tis the fetter'd soul's releasing :
    Weep not for me.

When the pangs of death assail me,
    Weep not for me :
Christ is mine,—He cannot fail me,
    Weep not for me :
Yes, though sin and doubt endeavour
From his love my soul to sever,
Jesus is my strength for ever !
    Weep not for me.

DALE.

MY TIMES ARE IN THY HAND.

"My times are in thy hand,"
My God ! I wish them there ;
My life, my friends, my soul, I leave
Entirely to thy care.

"My times are in thy hand,"
Whatever they may be ;
Pleasing or painful, dark or bright,
As best may seem to Thee.

"My times are in thy hand,"
Why should I doubt or fear ?
My Father's hand will never cause
His child a needless tear.

"My times are in thy hand,"—
Jesus the crucified !
The hand my cruel sins had pierced
Is now my guard and guide.

" My times are in thy hand,"—·
I'll always trust in Thee ;
And after death at thy right hand
I shall for ever be.

ANON.

REST ABOVE.

Here I find no rest ;
By fierce pain opprest,
And by sin distrest,
      I am weary, weary !

Though this world be fair,
Sin is ever there,
And its guilt I share :
      I am weary, weary !

Soon death's night will come,—
Where is now the gloom
Of the silent tomb ?
      I am weary, weary !

Christ hath died to prove
God's amazing love.
O for life above !
      I am weary, weary !

Earth gives me no pleasure ;
Heaven contains my treasure,—
Bliss in boundless measure :
   I am weary, weary !

Why should I complain ?
Jesus suffer'd pain,
And for me was slain :
   I am weary, weary !

Now, from heaven on high,
Christ hath heard my sigh,
Mark'd my mournful cry :
   I am weary, weary !

He hath given me peace,
Even tho' pains increase,
Soon shall sorrow cease :
   I am weary, weary !

Dawn thou heav'nly light,
On my ravished sight ;
All there's pure and bright !
   I am weary, weary !

       Anon.

WINGS LIKE A DOVE.

My soul, amid this stormy world,
  Is like some flutter'd dove;
And fain would be as swift of wing,
  To flee to Him I love.
The cords that bound my heart to earth
  Are broken by his hand:
Before his cross I found myself,
  A stranger in the land.

That visage marr'd, those sorrows deep,
  The vinegar and gall,
Were Jesus' golden chains of love
  His captive to enthrall!
My heart is with Him on his throne,
  And ill can brook delay;
Each moment list'ning for the voice,—
  "Rise up and come away."

With hope deferr'd, oft sick and faint,
  "Why tarries He?" I cry:
And should my Saviour chide my haste,
  Sure I could make reply.
May not an exile, Lord, desire,
  His own sweet land to see?
May not a captive seek release,
  A pris'ner to be free?

A child, when far away, may long
  For home and kindred dear;
And she that wails her absent Lord
  May sigh till he appear.
I would, my Lord and Saviour, know,
  That which no measure knows;
Would search the mystery of thy love,—
  The depth of all thy woes.

SIR E. DENNY.

ONWARD.

We go with the redeem'd to taste
   Of joy supreme, that never dies ;
Our feet still press the weary waste,
   Our hearts, our home, are in the skies.

And oh ! while on to Zion's hill
   The toilsome path of life we tread,
Around us, loving Father, still
   Thy circling wings of mercy spread.

From day to day, from hour to hour,
   Oh ! let our rising spirits prove
The strength of thine Almighty pow'r—
   The sweetness of thy saving love.

Anon.

HOW LONG?

My God, it is not fretfulness
    That makes me say "how long?"
It is not heaviness of heart
    That hinders me in song;
'Tis not despair of truth and right,
    Nor coward dread of wrong.

But how can I, with such a hope
    Of glory and of home;
With such a joy before my eyes,
    Not wish the time were come,—
Of years the jubilee, of days
    The Sabbath and the sum?

These years, what ages they have been?
    This life, how long it seems?
And how can I, in evil days,
    'Mid unknown hills and streams,
But sigh for those of home and heart,
    And visit them in dreams?

Yet peace, my heart, and hush, my tongue ;
　Be calm my troubled breast ;
Each restless hour is hastening on
　The everlasting rest :
Thou knowest that the time thy God
　Appoints for thee, is best.

Let faith, not fear nor fretfulness,
　Awake the cry, " how long ?"
Let no faint-heartedness of soul
　Damp thy aspiring song :
Right comes, truth dawns, the night departs
　Of error and of wrong.

H. Bonar.

WE SHALL ARISE.

High lies the better country,
The land of morning and perpetual spring ;
But graciously the warder
Over its mountain-border
Leans to us, beckoning,—bids us, "Come up hither!"
And, though we climb with step unfixed and slow,
From visioning heights of hope we look off thither.
And we must go.

Beloved ! beloved ! not cloud and fire alone
From bondage and the wilderness restore,
And guide the wandering spirit to its own ;
But all His elements, they go before :
Upon its way the seasons bring,
And hearten with foreshadowing
The resurrection-wonder, ·
What lands of death awake to sing
And germs of hope swell under !
And full and fine, and full and fine,
The day distils life's golden wine ;

And night is Palace Beautiful, peace-chambered.
All things are ours ; and life fills up of them
    Such measure as we hold.
      For ours beyond the gate,
    The deep things, the untold,
      We only wait.

ANON.

MOUNTAIN AND VALLEY.

On Alpine heights the love of God is shed;
    He plants the morning red,
    The flowerets white and blue,
    And feeds them with his dew.
On Alpine heights a loving Father dwells.

On Alpine heights, o'er many a fragrant heath,
    The loveliest breezes breathe;
    So free and pure the air,
    His breath seems floating there.
On Alpine heights a loving Father dwells.

On Alpine heights, beneath his mild blue eye,
    Still vales and meadows lie;
    The soaring glacier's ice
    Gleams like a paradise.
On Alpine heights a loving Father dwells.

Down Alpine heights the silvery streamlets flow,
   There the bold chamois go ;
   On giddy crags they stand,
   And drink from his own hand.
On Alpine heights a loving Father dwells.

On Alpine heights, in troops all white as snow,
   The sheep and wild goats go ;
   There, in the solitude,
   He fills their heart with food.
On Alpine heights a loving Father dwells.

On Alpine heights the herdsman tends his herd ;
   His shepherd is the Lord ;
   For He who feeds the sheep
   Will sure his offspring keep.
On Alpine heights a loving Father dwells.

KRUMMACHER.

THE GUEST.

Speechless sorrow sat with me ;
I was sighing wearily !
Lamp and fire were out ; the rain
Wildly beat the window pane.
In the dark we heard a knock,
And a hand was on the lock ;
One in waiting spake to me,
   Saying sweetly,
" I am come to sup with thee !"

All my room was dark and damp ;
" Sorrow," said I, " trim the lamp ;
Light the fire, and cheer thy face ;
Set the guest-chair in its place."
And again I heard the knock :
In the dark I found the lock—
" Enter, I have turned the key !
   Enter, stranger,
Who art come to sup with me !"

Opening wide the door He came ;
But I could not speak his name ;
In the guest-chair took his place,
But I could not see his face ;
When my cheerful fire was beaming,
When my little lamp was gleaming,
And the feast was spread for three,
   Lo ! my Master
Was the guest that supped with me !

HARRIET M'EWEN KIMBALL.

ARISE.

Arise,
My soul, arise !
Sing with thy latest breath
Christ's conquest over death.
Arise,
My soul, arise !
Sing it unto the skies.
Sing it over the earth and under ;
There, 'mongst the myriad graves
Of kings or slaves,
Let the song pierce their urns asunder.
Arise,
Our souls, arise !
In heaven, the angel-band
Stand ready, in each hand
A palm to wave ;
On earth, a listening throng
Wait the redeeming song,
Their souls to save.

Below, all silently,
The dead attend the cry :
  O grave !
Where is thy victory ?
  The branches wave ;
Our Lord hath risen on high !
  O death !
Where is thy sting ?
  The dust beneath
Stirs while we sing.
O grave ! where is thy victory ?
O death ! where is thy sting ?
  Arise,
  Our souls, arise !

    Mrs. Sarah Flower Adams.

WHOM HAVING NOT SEEN YE LOVE.

How strange is Heavenly Love !
  I never saw his face,
I never trod his courts above,
  I have but known his grace,
Yet my affections cling
  To his beloved side,
I feel He is my God, my King,
  And I his ransomed bride.

How strong is Heavenly Love !
  Stronger than ought below,
Though wide and wild my passions rove,
  I will not let Him go ;
What though I see Him not,
  I feel the ardour burn,
He hath for me the victory wrought,
  I love Him in return.

How sweet is Heavenly Love !
  'Tis all in all to me,

I muse on Him in field and grove,
   Or sailing o'er the sea.
I walk with Jesus here
   Not lonely though alone,
Till in his presence I appear,
   And know as I am known.

ANON.

HASTE NOT—REST NOT.

"WITHOUT haste ! without rest !"
Bind the motto to thy breast !
Bear it with thee as a spell ;
Storm or sunshine, guard it well ;
Heed not flowers that round thee bloom—
Bear it onward to the tomb !

Haste not—let no thoughtless deed
Mar fore'er the spirit's speed ;
Ponder well and know the right,
Onward then with all thy might :
Haste not—years can ne'er atone
For one reckless action done !

Rest not !—life is sweeping by,
Go and dare before you die ;
Something mighty and sublime
Leave behind to conquer time ;

Glorious 'tis to live for aye
When these forms have passed away.

" Haste not !—rest not !"   Calmly wait ;
Meekly bear the storms of fate ;
Duty be thy polar guide ;
Do the right, whate'er betide !
Haste not !—rest not !   Conflicts past,
God shall crown thy work at last !

GOETHE.

OUR REST.

My feet are worn and weary with the march
  Over rough roads and up the steep hill-side;
Oh, city of our God, I fain would see
  Thy pastures green, where peaceful waters glide.

My hands are weary, labouring, toiling on,
  Day after day, for perishable meat;
Oh, city of our God, I fain would rest;
  I sigh to gain thy glorious mercy-seat.

My garments, travel-worn and stained with dust,
  Oft rent by briars and thorns that crowd my way,
Would fain be made, O Lord, my righteousness,
  Spotless and white in heaven's unclouded ray.

My eyes are weary looking at the sin,
  Impiety, and scorn upon the earth;
Oh, city of our God, within thy walls,
  All, all are clothed upon with the new birth.

My heart is weary of its own deep sin—
  Sinning, repenting, sinning still alway;
When shall my soul thy glorious presence feel,
  And find its guilt, dear Saviour, washed away?

Patience, poor soul; the Saviour's feet were worn;
  The Saviour's heart and hands were weary too;
His garments stained and travel-worn and old,
  His sacred eyes blinded with tears for you.

Love thou the path of sorrow that he trod;
  Toil on, and wait in patience for thy rest;
Oh, city of our God, we soon shall see
  Thy glorious walls, home of the loved and blest.

S. ROBERTS.

WE WOULD SEE JESUS !

We would see Jesus—for the shadows lengthen
    Across the little landscape of our life :
We would see Jesus, our weak faith to strengthen
    For the last weariness, the final strife.

We would see Jesus—for life's hand hath rested,
    With its dark touch upon both heart and brow,
And though our souls have many a billow breasted
    Others are rising in the distance now.

We would see Jesus—other lights are paling
    Which for long years we have rejoiced to see ;
The blessings of our pilgrimage are failing,
    We will not mourn them—for we go to thee.

We would see Jesus—the great rock foundation
    Whereon our feet were set by sovereign grace ;
Not life, nor death, with all their agitation
    Can thence remove us if we see his face.

We would see Jesus—yet the spirit lingers
  Round the dear objects it has loved so long,
And earth from earth can scarce unclose its fingers;
  Our love to Thee makes not this love less strong.

We would see Jesus—sense is all too blinding,
  And heaven appears too dim, too far away.
We would see Thee, to gain a sweet reminding
  That Thou hast promised our great debt to pay.

We would see JESUS—this is all we're needing,
  Strength, joy, and willingness come with the sight;
We would see Jesus, dying, risen, pleading,
  Then welcome day and farewell mortal night.

AMERICAN.

A BROKEN HEART.

Oh! blessed be the heart that breaks!
  It is a broken heart that wins
The fellowship of Him who takes
  Our sorrows with our sins!

As many a flower has blown and blush'd,
  Yet ne'er its hidden sweets distill'd
Until its bleeding leaves were crush'd,
  And gather'd dews were spill'd;

So many a heart, that ne'er requites
  Its Father's love, perchance may need
That He should pluck its green delights,
  Or bruise it so it bleed!

Oft, thus, what we had thought to keep,
  He takes—to make it ours the more;
And calls our heavy eyes to weep
  That ne'er knew tears before;

Or warns us first with wounding dart,
    Then smites us with his chastening rod ;
Till, when we have a broken heart,
    We yield it up to God !

T. T.

EVENING SONG AFTER A DAY OF DIFFICULTY.

Lord, a happy child of thine,
   Patient through the love of Thee,
In the light, the life divine,
   Lives, and walks at liberty.

Leaning on thy tender care,
   Thou hast led my soul aright;
Fervent was my morning prayer,
   Joyful is my song to-night.

Oh, my Saviour, Guardian true,
   All my life is thine to keep;
At thy feet my work I do,
   In thy arms I fall asleep.

Tender mercies on my way,
   Falling softly like the dew,
Sent me freshly every day,
   I will bless the Lord for you.

Though I have not all I would,
  Though to greater bliss I go,
Every present gift of good
  To eternal love I owe.

Source of all that comforts me,
  Well of joy for which I long,
Let the song I sing to thee,
  Be an everlasting song.

MRS. WARING.

LIKE CHRIST.

BE it my anxious care to know
If more like Christ I daily grow,
   If He, my Lord, dwell in my heart,
If ever towards the mark I press,
   And never from his path depart.

If still in Christ I walk and live,
If as a goodly branch I thrive,
   And draw from Jesus strength and power
If when my heart is sore distressed,
When it complains, with grief oppressed,
   I come to Christ at every hour.

If I neglect through carelessness
My duty, or through weariness,
   Or my frail heart inconstant be :
If I, each day, all outward sin,
And treachery that lurks within,
   Repent in all sincerity.

If Christ to me is all in all ;
If still, whate'er on earth befall,
 My source of blessedness is this,
Beneath his gracious smile to live.
If evermore I wrestling strive,
 To be the Lord's and only his.

THOLUCK.

"SHE IS NOT DEAD, BUT SLEEPETH."

THE baby wept;
The mother took it from the nurse's arms,
And soothed its griefs, and still'd its vain alarms,
And baby slept.

Again it weeps,
And God doth take it from the mother's arms,
From present pain, and future unknown harms,
And baby sleeps.

DR. HINDS.

HOME OF THE CONQUERORS.

HOME of the conquerors ! how bright,
How glorious shine thy walls of light !
May I, through Christ, a passage win,
And, late or early, enter in.

No clang of arms, no shouts are there,
Borne on the soft and balmy air ;
No snares are spread, no serpent's fold,
Upon the shining streets of gold.

No foeman's form is there descried,
No whisper heard of hate or pride ;
To all the storms that *here* may swell,
The hosts of heaven have bid farewell.

O joy ! when all our fear and ill
Shall cease with Jesu's " Peace, be still."
O joy ! when we shall sin no more,
But holy live for evermore.

Home of the conquerors ! I press
Towards thy haunts of happiness.
In Jesu's name I fight, I win ;
Lift up the gates and let me in !

E. A. W.

OUR BELOVED.

Our beloved have departed,
While we tarry, broken-hearted,
    In the dreary, empty house.
They have ended life's brief story,
They have reached the home of glory,
    Over death victorious.

Hush that sobbing, weep more lightly,
On we travel, daily, nightly,
    To the rest that they have found.
Are we not upon the river,
Sailing fast to meet for ever
    On more holy, happy ground?

  *   *   *   *   *

On we haste, to home invited,
There with friends to be united
    In a surer land than here;
Meeting soon;—and meet for ever!

Glorious hope ! Forsake us never,
    For thy glimmering light is dear.

Ah ! the way is shining clearer,
As we journey ever nearer
    To the everlasting home.
Comrades ! who await our landing !
Friends ! who round the throne are standing !
    We salute you, and we come.

LANGE.

THE REFUGE.

Mortal, who sittest silent, dumb with woe,
Know'st thou to whom the sorrowful should go?
Hast thou not heard of One who lived and died
To bless mankind, Jesus, the crucified?
Shake off thy lethargy; to Jesus flee:
" Be of good comfort; rise, He calleth thee."

Oh, not in vain was the Redeemer sent,
Nor vain the years of grief and toil he spent;
It was to teach us how to bear the rod,
To suffer and to do the will of God.
Mortal, shake off thy gloom; to Jesus flee:
" Be of good comfort; rise, He calleth thee."

Our Saviour never shrank from duty's call,
He gave for sinful man his life, his all;
Mortal, he thought no pain too great for you,
And is there nothing thou canst find to do?
Ah, yield not to despair; to Jesus flee:
" Be of good comfort; rise, He calleth thee."

Thou hast been creeping slowly o'er the road
That leads to peace, to purity, to God ;
And now a hand is stretched to lead thee on,
'Twill ne'er forsake thee till the goal is won.
Oh, thrust it not away ; to Jesus flee :
" Be of good comfort ; rise, he calleth thee."

Thou hast been sitting by the way-side blind,
And never any healer could'st thou find ;
But hearing now that Jesus passeth by,
To Him with earnest heart and voice you cry ;
And He has heard thee ! then to Jesus flee :
" Be of good comfort ; rise, He calleth thee."

ANON.

WHEN HE GIVETH QUIETNESS, WHO THEN CAN MAKE TROUBLE?

Quiet from God! how beautiful to keep
   This treasure the All-merciful hath given,
To feel when we awake and when we sleep,
   This incense round us, like a breath from heaven.

To sojourn in the world, and yet apart;
   To dwell with God, and still with man to feel;
To bear about for ever in the heart
   The gladness which his Spirit doth reveal.

Who shall make trouble then?   Not evil minds,
   Which like a shadow o'er creation lower.
The soul which peace hath thus attuned finds
   How strong within doth reign the Calmer's power.

What shall make trouble?   Not slow-wasting pain,
   Nor even the threatening, certain stroke of death.
These do but wear away, then break the chain
   Which bound the spirit down to things beneath.

Anon.

MATTHEW XX. 17–28.

THY thoughts were on Jerusalem,
   The cross before *thine* eye ;
But Thou, O Lord, didst look in vain
   For human sympathy.

Thy thoughts were on the many things
   That Thou should'st suffer there ;
While thy disciples only thought
   Of glory as their share.

Thy thoughts were on the crown of thorns,
   The grief, the shame, the woe ;
Their thoughts were on the glorious crowns
   Thou would'st on them bestow.

How selfish is the human heart !
   (O God, we feel, and own),
That, while the Saviour seeks a *cross*,
   Can seek *itself* a *throne*.

A. A. W.

GOD EVERYWHERE.

O THOU, by long experience tried,
Near whom no grief can long abide :
My Lord, how full of sweet content
I pass my years of banishment !

All scenes alike engaging prove
To souls impress'd with sacred love.
Where'er they dwell, they dwell in Thee :
In heaven, in earth, or on the sea.

To me remains nor place nor time,
My country is in every clime ;
I can be calm and free from care
On any shore, since God is there.

While place we seek, or place we shun,
The soul finds happiness in none ;
But with a God to guide our way,
'Tis equal joy to go or stay.

Could I be cast where Thou art not,
That were indeed a dreadful lot;
But regions none remote I call,
Secure of finding God in all.

GUION.

THE RETROSPECT.

When the vale of death appears,
   Faint and cold this mortal clay,
Kind Forerunner, soothe my fears,
   Light me through the darksome way :
     Break the shadows,
   Usher in eternal day.

Starting from this dying state,
   Upward bid my soul aspire ;
Open thou the crystal gate,
   To thy praise attune my lyre :
     Dwell for ever,—
   Dwell on each immortal wire.

From the sparkling turrets there,
   Oft I'll trace my pilgrim way ;
Often bless thy guardian care,—
   Fire by night, and cloud by day,—
     While my triumphs
   At my Leader's feet I lay.

And when mighty trumpets blown
Shall the judgment dawn proclaim,
From the central burning throne,
'Mid creation's final flame,
With the ransom'd,
Judge and Saviour, own my name !

MRS. GILBERT.

WORK AND REST.

WHAT have I yet to do ?
  Day weareth on—
Flowers that, opening new,
Smile through the morning's dew,
  Droop in the sun.

'Neath the noon's scorching glare,
  Fainting I stand ;
Still is the sultry air,
Silentness everywhere
  Through the hot land.

Yet must I labour still,
  All the day through—
Striving with earnest will,
Patient my place to fill,
  My work to do.

Long though my task may be,
  Cometh the end.
God 'tis that helpeth me,
His is the work, and He
  New strength will lend.

He will direct my feet,
  Strengthen my hand ;
Give me my portion meet ;
Firm in his promise sweet
  Trusting I'll stand.

Up, then, to work again !
  God's word is given,
That none shall sow in vain,
But find his ripened grain,
  Garnered in heaven.

Larger the shadows fall,
  Night cometh on ;
Low voices softly call, ·
" Come, here is rest for all !
  Labour is done !"

ANON.

THE HARVEST HOME.

From the far-off fields of earthly toil,
  A goodly host they come ;
And sounds of music are on the air,
  'Tis the song of the Harvest Home !
The weariness and the weeping,
  The darkness, has all passed by,
And a glorious sun has risen,
  The sun of eternity !

We've seen those faces in days of yore,
  When the dust was on their brow,
And the scalding tear upon their cheek ;
  Let us look at the lab'rers now !
We think of the life-long sorrow,
  And the wilderness days of care ;
We try to trace the tear-drops ;
  But no scars of grief are there !

There's a mystery of soul-chastened joy
   Lit up with sunlight hues,
Like morning flowers, *most* beautiful
   When wet with midnight dews.
There are depths of earnest meaning
   In each true and trustful gaze,
Telling of wondrous lessons
   Learnt in their pilgrim days;

And a conscious confidence of bliss,
   That shall never again remove;
All the faith and hope of journeying years
   Gathered up in that look of love!
The long waiting days are over,
   They've received their wages now;
For they've gazed upon their Master,
   And his name is on their brow.

They have seen the safely garner'd sheaves,
   And the song has been passing sweet,
Which welcomed the last incoming one
   Laid down at the Saviour's feet.
Oh, well does *his* heart remember,
   As those notes of praise sweep by,
The yearning, plaintive music
   Of earth's sadder minstrelsy!

And well does *He* know each chequer'd tale,
  As He looks on the joyous band;
All the lights and shadows that cross'd their path
  In the distant pilgrim land;
The heart's unspoken anguish,
  The bitter sighs and tears,
The long, long hours of watching,
  The changeful hopes and fears !

One had climbed the rugged mountain side—
  'Twas a bleak and wintry day—
The tempest had scattered his precious seed,
  And he wept as he turned away.
But a stranger hand had watered
  That seed on a distant shore,
And the lab'rers now are meeting,
  Who had never met before.

And *one*—he had toiled amid burning sands
  When the scorching sun was high ;
He had grasped the plough with a fever'd hand,
  And then laid him down to die !
But another, and yet another,
  Had filled that deserted field ;
Nor vainly the seed they scatter'd
  Where a brother's care had tilled.

Some with eager steps went boldly forth,
   Broad-casting o'er the land ;
Some watered the scarcely budding blade
   With a tender, gentle hand.
There's one—her young life was blighted
   By the withering touch of woe ;
Her days were sad and weary,
   And *she* never went forth to sow.

But there rose from her lonely couch of pain
   The fervent pleading prayer ;
She looks on many a radiant brow,
   And she reads the answer *there !*
Yes ! sowers and reapers are meeting,
   A rejoicing host they come :
Will *you* join the echoing chorus ?
   'Tis the song of the Harvest Home !

C. P.

HYMN.

No ! no !   It is not dying
  To Jesus' self to go ;
The gloom of earth forsaking,
In one's pure home awaking,
  Should give no pang of woe.

No ! no !   It is not dying,
  In heaven at last to dwell ;
In the eternal glory
Of crown and harp and story
  Our earthly fears to quell.

No ! no !   It is not dying,
  To hear the gracious tone
Of the Almighty, saying :
" Come, child, wherever straying,
  Behold me on the throne ! "

No! no!   It is not dying,
  To leave this world of strife,
And seek that blessed river,
Where Christ shall lead for ever,
  His sheep 'neath trees of life.

No! no!   It is not dying,
  With lordly glory crown'd,
To join in the thanksgiving
To Him, the everliving,
  With which the heavens resound.

O no!   It is not dying,
  Thou Saviour of thine own!
There from the fount Eternal,
Gush life and joy supernal;
  Here there are drops alone.

GERHARDT.

DESIRE TO DEPART.

LET me depart, beloved, I entreat ye !
  Oh ! I am weary of these mortal bands.
Know ye *who* waits upon the throne to greet me ?
  What voice has called me to celestial lands ?

Hinder me not ; your loving ministrations
  Do but bind up this shattered house of clay ;
When my poor heart with agonized pulsations
  Has nearly worn the crumbling walls away.

See how it flutters, in the vain endeavour ;
  Hear the hard labour of my panting breath.
" How long, O Lord, how long ! oh, wilt thou never
  Lend to my help thy strong deliv'rer, Death ? "

Think not, beloved, that I measure lightly
  All your long patience, your unwearied care ;
The tender love that kept its vigils nightly,
  Whilst hope sank slowly into long despair.

For, when the message to my soul was spoken :
  "Thy work is finished ; thou art called above ;
Herewith I give to thee a certain token "—
  Ah ! I clung sobbing to my earthly love.

But day by day have faith and hope waxed stronger,
  Till now, that my Redeemer bids me come,
My soul exults ; I would not tarry longer
  Far from the shelter of my Father's home.

Jordan is wide ; its stormy billows gather ;
  My mortal weakness shudders at their strength ;
But, on the other side, I know my Father
  Waits to receive me into rest, at length.

I near the shore—thanks for a faith unshaken ;
  Jesus has kept me in his close embrace.
" Good night," beloved ; when again I waken
  I shall indeed behold Him " face to face !"

ANON.

REST, WEARY SOUL.

Rest, weary soul !
The penalty is borne, the ransom paid,
For all thy sins full satisfaction made ;
Strive not thyself to do what Christ has done :
Take the free gift, and make the joy thine own.
No more by pangs of guilt and fear distrest—
Rest, sweetly rest.

Rest, weary heart !
From all thy silent griefs, and secret pain,
Thy profitless regrets and longings vain ;
Wisdom and love have ordered all the past,
All shall be blessedness and light at last :
Cast off the cares that have so long opprest—
Rest, sweetly rest.

Rest, weary head !
Lie down to slumber in the peaceful tomb,
Light from above has broken through its gloom ;

Here, in the place where once thy Saviour lay,
Where He shall wake thee on a future day,
Like a tired child upon its mother's breast—
    Rest, sweetly rest.

    Rest, spirit free !
In the green pasture of the heavenly shore,
Where sin and sorrow can approach no more ;
With all the flock by the good Shepherd fed,
Beside the streams of life eternal led,
For ever with thy God and Saviour blest—
    Rest, sweetly rest.

ANON.

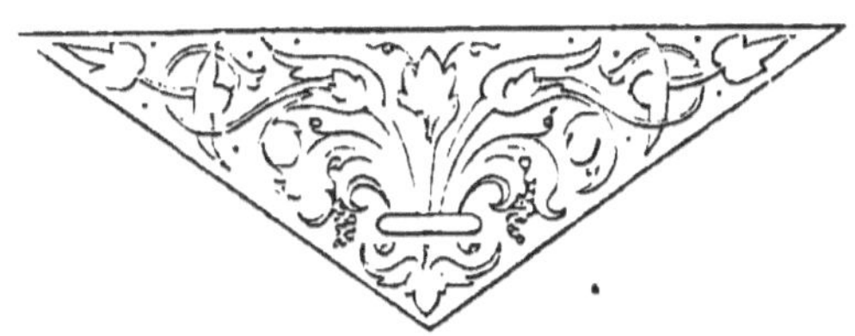

HOW LONG?

THE tear will fall, O Father,
    When I see
Those curious glances
    Fixed on me.
How long this cross, my Saviour, must I bear?
" Until thine eyes no more can shed a tear."

The flush will rise, O Father,
    When I hear
Those rude, insulting words—
    The bitter jeer.
How long, O Lord, must I, with trembling, fear?
"Till thou these mocking words no more canst hear!"

Sad are my thoughts, O Father,
    Well I know,
Ofttimes neglects are mine,
    From this deep woe.
How long, kind Parent, must I check each sob?
" Until thy heart no more with pain can throb."

Then all my life, O Father,
    Teach me how,
  Beneath this galling cross
    To humbly bow.
Oh! shall I never cease to feel thy rod?
" All trials cease in heaven, at home with God !"

ANON.

THOU WILT NEVER GROW OLD.

Thou wilt never grow old,
   Nor weary, nor sad in the home of thy birth ;
My beautiful lily, thy leaves will unfold
   In a clime that is purer and brighter than earth ;
O holy and fair, I rejoice thou art there,
   In that kingdom of light, with its cities of gold ;
Where the air thrills with angel hosannas and where
     Thou wilt never grow old, sweet—
      Never grow old !

I am a pilgrim, with sorrow and sin
   Haunting my footsteps wherever I go,
Life is a warfare my title to win—
   Well will it be if it end not in woe.
Pity me, sweet, I am laden with care ;
   Dark are my garments with mildew and mould ;
Thou, my bright angel, art sinless and fair,
     And wilt never grow old, sweet—
      Never grow old !

Now, canst thou hear from thy home in the skies,
    All the fond words I am whispering to thee?
Dost thou look down on me with the soft eyes
    Greeting me oft ere thy spirit was free?
So I believe, though the shadows of time
    Hide the bright spirit I yet shall behold;
Thou wilt still love me, and, pleasure sublime,
        Thou wilt never grow old, sweet—
           Never grow old.

Thus wilt thou be when the pilgrim, grown gray,
    Weeps when the vines from the hearthstone are
        riven;
Faith shall behold thee, as pure as the day
    Thou wert torn from the earth and transplanted
        to heaven.
O holy and fair, I rejoice thou art there,
    In that kingdom of light, with its cities of gold,
Where the air thrills with angel hosannas, and where
        Thou wilt never grow old, sweet—
           Never grow old!   ·

MRS. HOWARTH.

UPHELD.

When heart and flesh despondent sink
And from life's warfare fain would shrink,
An upward glance brings heavenly cheer;
Upheld by Him I smile at fear.

When life appears a sea of woe,
And all its waves my soul o'erflow,
To Him I flee for sure relief;
Upheld by Him, I smile at grief.

When troubles like a mountain rise,
And comfort from my bosom flies,
I to the mercy-seat repair;
Upheld by Him, I smile at care,

When earthly treasure fails and fades,
And chilling poverty invades,
He every needed good will grant;
Upheld by Him, I smile at want.

When faith grows dim, and from its sight
My star of hope would vail its light,
Grace bids a beam of joy shine out :
Upheld by Him, I smile at doubt.

When wasting anguish and disease
Upon my suffering body seize,
My murmuring lips shall not complain :
Upheld by Him, I smile at pain.

When time with me shall reach its close,
And in the grave I seek repose,
With joy I'll yield my failing breath ;
Upheld by Him, I smile at death.

ANON.

FAITH.

SEE Faith, with upward eyes,
Beholds the distant land ;
Her fair possessions in the skies,
And waits with outstretched hand.

She leans upon the cross,
And sheds a tear or two :
But glory plays in either eye,
As beams in early dew.

She smiles in deep distress,
In storms she stands serene ;
The whirlwind idly rages by,
Unmoved she views the scene.

The world beneath her feet,
She heeds not, or disdains ;
Her thundering foes are slain, or bound
In adamantine chains.

She waits the voice of God,
That calls her to the skies ;
Then soars aloft, in glory veiled,
And in fruition dies.

LAWSON.

THOUGHTS IN BLINDNESS.

O LOSS of sight, of thee I most complain !
Blind among enemies, O worse than chains,
Dungeon, or beggary, or decrepit age !
Light, the prime work of God, to me is extinct,
And all her various objects of delight
Annull'd, which might in part my grief have
     eas'd,
Inferior to the vilest now become
Of man or worm ; the vilest here excel me :
They creep, yet see ; I, dark in light, expos'd
To daily fraud, contempt, abuse, and wrong,
Within doors, or without, still as a fool,
In power of others, never in my own ;
Scarce half I seem to live, dead more than half.
Oh, dark, dark, dark, amid the blaze of noon,
Irrecoverably dark, total eclipse
    Without all hope of day !
O first created beam, and thou great Word,

" Let there be light, and light was over all ;"
Why am I thus bereav'd thy prime decree?
    The sun to me is dark
    And silent as the moon,
    When she deserts the night,
Hid in her vacant interlunar cave.

MILTON.

THE PILGRIM'S FAREWELL.

Farewell, poor world! I must be gone;
Thou art no home, no rest for me:
I'll take my staff, and travel on,
Till I a better world may see.

Why art thou loth, my heart? O why
Dost thou recoil within my breast?
Grieve not, but say farewell, and fly
Unto the ark, my dove! there's rest.

I come, my Lord, a pilgrim's pace;
Weary and weak, I slowly move;
Longing, but can't yet reach the place,
The gladsome place of rest above.

I come, my Lord, the floods here rise,
These troubled seas foam nought but mire;
My dove back to my bosom flies:
Farewell, poor world!—heaven's my desire.

"Stay, stay," said Earth, "whither, fond one?
Here's a fair world, what would'st thou have?"
Fair world!   Oh no, thy beauty's gone,
A heavenly Canaan, Lord, I crave.

Thus ancient travellers,—thus they,
Weary of earth, sighed after thee :
They're gone before,—I may not stay,
Till I both thee and them may see.

Put on, my soul, put on with speed ;
Though the way be long, the end is sweet :
Once more, poor world, farewell indeed !
In leaving thee, my Lord I meet.

ANON.

RACHEL'S TEARS.

OH, weep not o'er thy children's tomb,
 O Rachel, weep not so !
The bud is cropped by martyrdom,
 The flower in heaven shall blow !

Firstlings of faith ! the murderer's knife
 Has missed its deadliest aim :
The God for whom they gave their life,
 For them to suffer came !

Though feeble were their days and few,
 Baptised in blood and pain,
He knows them, whom they never knew,
 And they shall live again.

Then weep not o'er thy children's tomb,
 O Rachel, weep not so !
The bud is cropped by martyrdom,
 The flower in heaven shall blow.

HEBER.

THE HEAVENLY WELL-SPRING.

Bliss beyond compare,
Which in Christ I share !
He's my only joy and treasure ;
Tasteless is all worldly pleasure,
When in Christ I share
Bliss beyond compare.

Jesus is my joy,
Therefore, blest am I.
Oh ! his mercy is unbounded,
All my hope on Him is founded ;
Jesus is my joy,
Therefore blest am I.

When the Lord appears,
This my spirit cheers ;
When, his love to me revealing,
He, the Sun of Grace, with healing
In his beams, appears,—
This my Spirit cheers.

Then all grief is drown'd ;
Pure delight is found.
Joy and peace in his salvation,
Heav'nly bliss and consolation,
Ev'ry grief is drown'd
Where such bliss is found.

ANON.

OUR EVERLASTING HOME.

STILL in a world of sin and pain,
Far from our home, we meet again ;
Dreary and long our course may be,
But oh, our God, it leads to thee !
Thou art the light by which we roam,—
Thou art our everlasting home.

Thy hand is still around to bless,
Thou dost not leave us comfortless ;
Earth and its pain we still may feel,
But Thou art ever near to heal ;
Still as our day our strength shall be,
For all our cares are borne by Thee.

Still, as time's changing current rolls,
Thy comforts, Lord, delight our souls :
Thy mighty arm to smooth our way,
Thy light to turn our night to day ;
Onward with firmer steps we roam,
On to our everlasting home.

ANON.

BE STILL.

Be still, my soul ; Jehovah loveth thee ;
  Fret not nor murmur at thy weary lot ;
Though dark and lone thy journey seems to be,
  Be sure that thou art ne'er by Him forgot.
He ever loves ; then trust Him, trust Him still,
Let all thy care be this, the doing of his will.

Thy hand in his, like fondest, happiest child,
  Place thou, nor draw it for a moment thence ;
Walk thou with Him, a Father reconciled,
  Till in his own good time He call thee hence.
Walk with Him now, so shall thy way be bright,
And all thy soul be filled with his most glorious light.

Fight the good fight of faith, nor turn aside
  Through fear of peril from or earth or hell ;
Take to thee now the armour proved and tried,
  Take to thee spear and sword ;—oh, wield them
      well ;
So shalt thou conquer here, so win the day,
So wear the crown when this hard life has pass'd away.

Take courage ! faint not, though the foe be strong ;
  Christ is thy strength ; he fighteth on thy side ;
Swift be thy race ; remember, 'tis not long,
  The goal is near ; the prize He will provide ;
And then from earthly toil thou restest ever ;
Thy home on the fair banks of life's eternal river !

He comes with his reward ; 'tis just at hand ;
  He comes in glory to his promised throne.
My soul, rejoice ; ere long thy feet shall stand
  Within the city of the Blessed One.
Thy perils past, thy heritage secure,
Thy tears all wiped away, thy joy for ever sure.

H. BONAR.

LOOKING TO JESUS.

Thou, who didst stoop below,
To drain the cup of woe,
Wearing the form of frail mortality,—
Thy blessed labours done,
Thy crown of victory won,
Has passed from earth—passed to thy home on high.

Man may no longer trace
In thy celestial face,
The image of the bright, the viewless One;
Nor may thy servants hear,
Save with faith's raptured ear,
Thy voice of tenderness, God's holy Son!

Our eyes behold Thee not,
Yet hast Thou not forgot
Those who have placed their hope, their trust in
Thee;
Before thy Father's face
Thou hast prepared a place,
That where Thou art, there they may also be.

It was no path of flowers,
Through this dark world of ours,
Beloved of the Father, Thou didst tread ;
And shall we, in dismay,
Shrink from the narrow way,
When clouds and darkness are around it spread ?

O Thou, who art our life,
Be with us through the strife !
Was not thy head by earth's fierce tempest bowed ?
Raise Thou our eyes above,
To see a Father's love
Beam, like the bow of promise, through the cloud.

Even through the awful gloom,
Which hovers o'er the tomb,
That light of love our guiding star shall be ;
Our spirits shall not dread
The shadowy way to tread,
Friend, Guardian, Saviour, which doth lead to Thee.

ANON.

THE SECRET PLACE OF THE MOST HIGH.

Call Jehovah thy salvation,
  Rest beneath the Almighty's shade,
In his secret habitation
  Dwell, nor ever be dismay'd;
There no tumult can alarm thee,
  Thou shalt dread no hidden snare;
Guile nor violence can harm thee,
  In eternal safeguard there.

From the sword at noonday wasting,
  From the noisome pestilence
In the depth of midnight blasting,
  God shall be thy sure defence.
Fear not thou the deadly quiver,
  When a thousand feel the blow,
Mercy shall thy soul deliver,
  Though ten thousand be laid low.

Thee, though winds and waves be swelling
   God, thine hope, shall bear through all,
Plague shall not come near thy dwelling.
   Thee no evil shall befall ;
He shall charge his angel legions,
   Watch and guard o'er thee to keep,
Though thou walk through hostile regions,
   Though in desert wilds thou sleep.

Since, with pure and true affection,
   Thou on God hast set thy love,
With the wings of his protection
   He will shield thee from above :
Thou shalt call on Him in trouble,
   He will hearken, He will save ;
Here for grief reward thee double,
   Crown with life beyond the grave.

MONTGOMERY.

DEATH OF THE SAINT.

In vain our fancy strives to paint
   The moment after death,
The glories that surround the saint,
   When he resigns his breath.

One gentle sigh his fetters breaks;
   We scarce can say, " He's gone,"
Before the willing spirit takes
   Her mansion near the throne.

Faith strives, but all its efforts fail
   To trace her in her flight;
No eye can pierce within the veil,
   Which hides that world of light.

Thus much (and this is all) we know,
   They are supremely blest;
Have done with sin, and care, and woe,
   And with their Saviour rest.

On harps of gold they praise his name,
His face they always view;
Then let us followers be of them,
That we may praise him too.

NEWTON.

REST IN HOPE.

Rest, rest in hope, thou dying dust;
  Thou shalt arise in glory bright;
The grave shall hold thee but in trust :—
  God is the everlasting light
Of thee, and all the happy just.

COBBIN.

STAR OF MY HOPE.

STAR of my hope ! depart not ;
  My soul's supremest light ;
'Tis horror where thou art not,
  Worse than Egyptian night !

Though many a star of splendour
  Around the concave shine,
Their beams no comfort render,
  Till lighted up by thine !

But Thou, though far, canst lighten
  This dark world with thy ray ;
And, sunlike, heaven will brighten ;
  The fountain of its day !

EDMESTON.

I WOULD NOT LIVE ALWAYS.

Call earth an Eden, if on roses
    Your every step in life you tread ;
But he whose cherished all reposes
    Where rest the missing, silent dead,
Will have no wish to live for ever—
    Will deem each day too dearly won.
    Thank God, my five-and-thirtieth sun
Has passed !   Time, like this mountain river,
Rolls on.   Life hath for me few pleasures.
    Press lightly, earth, on my departed ;
    And soon shall I, the broken-hearted,
Lie down in rest where lie my treasures.

BÜRGER.

WHEN I AM DEAD.

When I am dead, and silent lying,
  Should you, in your hour of awe,
Gaze upon me, softly sighing,
  Back the solemn curtain draw:
But the frame of clay you'll see,
O belov'd, will not be me;
I shall be with Christ, my treasure,
Drinking in eternal pleasure.

When I'm in the coffin shrouded,
  Mantled in a winding-sheet,
All the springs of life beclouded,
  In that peaceable retreat:
Stay the tear; to weep forbear;
I, my friend, shall not be there;
I shall be where Sharon's Rose,
Chief in beauty, fragrant blows.

When you see my eye fast closed,
  And regret its quenched beam,—
Every fringy lash reposed
  Where oft flowed the copious stream :
Let no tear-drop fall from thine :
Dear one, it will not be mine ;
Mine on Jesus will be dwelling,
All the sons of light excelling !

When my feet, devoid of motion,
  Side by side inactive lay,
Should you think, with fond emotion,
  "Never more with me they'll stray !"
They will not be mine, beloved ;
Mine, by love's impatience moved,
Will o'er heaven's bright pavement glide,
Till they reach Immanuel's side.

Should your mournful eyebeam linger,
  Should your palm the surface press
Of my icy, marble finger,
  Shrinking from its nothingness :
Dearest friend, 'twill not be mine,
Motionless in palm of thine ;
Mine will then be sweetly playing,
O'er a harp angelic straying.

When you mark my head reposing,
  Heedless, thoughtless, tearless, still,
Death's dark victory disclosing,
  O'er the memory, heart, and will :
As you trace care's furrowed line
'Cross the brow, 'twill not be mine ;
Mine will lean on Jesus' breast,
Pillowed on eternal rest.

When the humid grave's receiving
  That cold casket, where to dwell,
Oft my spirit, sadly grieving,
  Found it but a prison cell :
I, my love, shall not be there,—
Clear escaped for ever, where
I shall then be with another,
Christ, my Lover, Bridegroom, Brother.

ANON.

HOMEWARD BOUND.

Out on an ocean all boundless we ride,
     We're homeward bound;
Tossed on the waves of a rough restless tide,
     We're homeward bound;
Far from the safe, quiet harbour we've rode,
Seeking our Father's celestial abode,
Promise of which on us each He bestowed,
     We're homeward bound.

Wildly the storm sweeps us on as it roars,
     We're homeward bound;
Look! yonder lie the bright heavenly shores,
     We're homeward bound;
Steady, O pilot! stand firm at the wheel,
Steady; we soon shall outweather the gale,
Oh, how we fly 'neath the loud creaking sail,
     We're homeward bound.

Into the harbour of heaven now we glide,
    We're home at last;
Softly we drift on its bright silver tide,
    We're home at last;
Glory to God! all our dangers are o'er;
We stand secure on the glorified shore;
Glory to God! we will shout evermore,
    We're home at last.

ANON.

A LITTLE WHILE.

A LITTLE while to walk this weary road ;
A little while to bear this heavy load ;
Then all our earthly pilgrimage shall cease,
And we shall wear the crown in perfect peace.

A little while to love with earthly love,
And then we share the " fulness " from above ;
A little time of darkness and of doubt,
Then the bright home whose light shall ne'er go out.

A little toil and sadness here below ;
A little time to watch, and plant, and sow ;
Then Jesus calls his labourers away,
Where everlasting joy and gladness stay.

A little while of storm, and wind, and rain,
And then the shining haven we shall gain ;
A little time to toss on life's rough sea,
Then in that peaceful home our rest shall be.

A little while !   O Saviour, make us strong
To bear that little, though it oft seem long :
Guide Thou our way with thine own loving hand,
Till we shall enter in the Promised Land !

NEW YORK OBSERVER.

A PRAYER.

FATHER ! for rest in Thee,
Toss'd on the heaving sea
Of my own fearful soul, I trembling cry !
Dark shadows round me fall,
Clouds brood on high o'er all,
And the night winds with mournful wail float by,
Whilst through the low'ring sky
Their voices sadly call.

Father ! for rest in Thee,
Under thy wing to be,
In thy protecting arm secure to lie,
To know that Thou art near,
And therefore not to fear
The chilling gusts that ceaselessly pass by—
Such is thy child's faint cry :
Father in heaven, hear !

This heart is faint and weak ;
This fragile reed must break,
But for the strength Thou only canst bestow.
Lord, let me trust in Thee—
Do thou my helper be—
The rock to shelter me from crushing woe ;
Teach me thy voice to know,
Thy hand in all to see !

Illume my future way
With a celestial ray
Drawn from thy heaven of peace, and love, and light ;
Let not the vain world dim
That ray, nor secret sin
O'ercloud its darkness to my spirit's sight ;
Throughout life's stormy night
Keep it unquenched within !

Let not my weak steps fail,
Let not my faint heart quail,
For his dear sake who agony hath known,
For his who bore our pain,
For his who shared our shame,
And trod the winepress of thy wrath alone,
That we might be his own,
Glory to his high name !

Father! oh, keep me still!
Through earthly good or ill,
Aid Thou my trembling feet to rest at last;
Oh, let the city bright,
Thy house be still in sight,
My beacon-star till death's dark wave is past!
Its harp-notes through the blast
Guide me to Thee aright!

M.

A RETROSPECT.

I SHOULD not mourn my passing youth,
If I had spent it, Lord, for Thee;
But oh, my coldness and untruth
Are oft a bitter grief to me!

The friends so early called away,
I would not wish them here again;
But would my soul had learnt to stay
More upon Thee, who dost remain!

I do not grieve that mine are not
The blessings I see others share;
But would my soul had ne'er forgot
The joy of which it is an heir!

No sorrow leaves a bitter taste;
'Tis only sin that can distress;
That I should time and talents waste,
Nor love Thee more, and this world less.

My years crowd sail, and pass away
Before me to eternity.
How poorly freighted, Lord, are they
With acts of faith and love to Thee !

O give me now a purer zeal ;
In true contrition keep me low ;
And any love that I may feel,
By meek obedience may I show.

Then, when life's little day is o'er,
I shall not mourn, its conflict won ;
The faithful servant asks no more
Than hear Thee say at last, " Well done ! "

E. A. W.

THINGS ABOVE.

STRONG is death's chilly blast,
Friends are departing fast,
Leaving the world to strangers and me,
Where all is so bitter cold.   Ah me ! the heart
　　grows old,
Long ere the dark locks whitened should be.

In many a dwelling the dread voice is telling,
That the bright eye is quenched, and the dark
　　coffin closed,
That chill, chill, and rigid now
Is that broad and beauteous brow,
Where thought and the sweetness of love once
　　reposed.

The tears cease to flow, the wild pulse of woe
For ever is hushed in the heart and the brain ;
Yet even from those lips, in death's dark eclipse,
They forbid us to weep.
We shall soon meet again.

Children of love and light,
Oh ! but your robes are bright :
Wore ye e'er the vestments of sin and of woe?
Oh, yes !   Then to Him, who did you redeem,
Let your high song of praise to eternity flow.

E. S.

DIVINE SHELTER.

Jesus ! most holy One !
   Pray I to Thee :
These chains of darkness,
   Lord, break for me !

Take this sad heart of mine,
   Mourning for sin,
To thy great heart of love !—
   Lord, take me in !

On the dark mountains
   Long have I strayed ;
Cold winds of sorrow
   Round me have played :

None to bring comfort—
   None have I found ;
Wild tears of anguish
   Watered the ground.

To this dear refuge
Now have I fled ;
Know I thy kind heart
For me has bled.

Take now the wanderer
Home to thy rest ;
Under thy kind wing
Sheltered and blest !

ANON.

JESUS HELP.

Oʜ, help me o'er this river,
    Thou who hast cross'd before ;
Oh help, or I shall never
    Reach the further shore.

Its waters swell and eddy ;
    I fall, I sink, I'm lost :
Oh keep my footsteps steady,
    Till I have safely cross'd.

Stretch out thy hand to save me,
    As Thou hast often done ;
For if *Thou* wilt not have me,
    Then I am wholly gone.

If *Thou*, dear Lord, wilt have me,
    If *Thou* wilt help my need ;
Ah, this will save, will save me,
    And I am saved indeed.

A word from *Thee* will do it,
  One word, one word, no more,
I shall be carried through it
  And landed on the shore.

Oh, help me through this trial,
  Thou tried and tempted One ;
I cannot take denial ;—
  Thou *must*, or I am gone.

'Tis Thee—Thee, Saviour, only,
  That can suffice for me ;
For I am tried and lonely,
  I have no friend but Thee.

ANON.

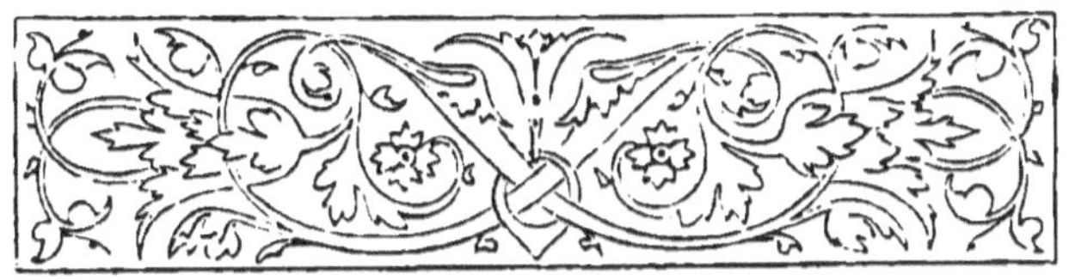

BE STRONG.

TAKE thy staff, O pilgrim,
    Haste thee on thy way;
Let the morrow find thee
    Farther than to-day.

If thou seek the city
    Of the Golden Street,
Pause not on thy pathway—
    Rest not, weary feet.

In the heavenly journey
    Press with zeal along;
Resting will but weary,
    Running make thee strong.

ANON.

CONSOLATION.

Where the mourner weeping
   Sheds the secret tear,
God his watch is keeping,
   Though none else be near.

Jesus ne'er will leave thee ;
   All thy wants He knows ;
Feels the pains that grieve thee,
   Sees thy hidden woes.

Raise thine eyes to heaven
   When thy spirits quail,
When, by tempests driven,
   Heart and courage fail.

When in grief we languish,
   He will dry the tear,
Who his children's anguish
   Soothes with succour near.

All our woe and sadness
In this world below,
Balance not the gladness
We in heaven shall know—

When our gracious Saviour,
In the realms above,
Crowns us with his favour,
Fills us with his love.   Amen.

ANON.

COMFORT IN AFFLICTION.

AFFLICTION is a stormy deep,
    Where wave resounds to wave;
Though o'er my head the billows roll,
    I know the Lord can save.

The hand which now withholds my joys,
    Can soon restore my peace;
And He, who bade the tempest rise,
    Can bid that tempest cease.

In the dark watches of the night,
    I'll count his mercies o'er;
I'll praise Him for ten thousand past,
    And humbly pray for more.

When darkness and when sorrow rose,
    And press'd on every side,
The Lord has still sustained my steps,
    And still has been my guide.

On Him I'll rest and build my hopes,
  Nor murmur at his rod ;
He's more than all the world to me,
  My health, my life, my God.

COTTON.

SECRET SORROWS.

DEEP in the heart's remotest cell
Lie hidden griefs and many a care,
Which e'en with those who love us well
We never can completely share.
Such pains can know no human cure,
From them no skill relief can find,
Life doth but teach us to endure
    The secret sorrows of the mind.

Though love may probe with cautious hand,
Though curiosity may pry,
The heart's dark mazes can't be scanned
By the most scrutinising eye.
Each one her bitterness best knows,
When her own anguish lies confined;
And bears apart as sacred woes,
    The secret sorrows of the mind.

One eye alone has marked our grief,
One voice has whispered hope and cheer,
One hand administered relief,
One heart in sympathy is near;
Yea none but He who formed the soul,
And first her place and powers defined,
Can turn to blessings or control
   The secret sorrows of the mind.

H. FRY.

THE ANVIL AND THE HAMMER.

For by afflictions, man refined growes,
And (as the gold prepared in the fire)
Receiveth such a forme by wrongs and blowes,
That he becomes the jewell we desire !
　　To Thee, therefore, O God ! my prayers are
Not to be freed from griefes and troubles quite ;
But, that they may be such as I can beare,
And serve to make me precious in thy sight.
　　This please me shall, though all my lifetime I
　　Between thine anvill and the hammer lie.

Wither.

HEAL ME.

GENTLY, gently lay thy rod
On my sinful head, O God.
Stay thy wrath, in mercy stay,
Lest I sink before its sway.

Heal me, for my flesh is weak ;
Heal me, for thy grace I seek ;
This my only plea I make,
Heal me for thy mercy's sake.

Who within the silent grave
Shall proclaim thy power to save ?
Lord, my trembling soul reprieve,
Speak, and I shall rise and live.

Lo ! He comes !   He heeds my plea !
Lo ! He comes ; the shadows flee !
Glory round me dawns once more ;
Rise, my spirit, and adore !

LYTE.

P

FAR FROM HOME.

FAR from home, I feel a longing ;
   Earth is but a barren clod ;
While the storms are round me thronging,
   Take, oh take me home to God.
Part, ye clouds of earth, asunder,
   Now I rise from this dull sod ;
Jesus, Lord, receive me yonder—
   Take, oh take me home to God.

AFFLICTION.

I CANNOT call affliction sweet,
   And yet 'twas good to bear ;
Affliction brought me to thy feet,
   And I found comfort there.

My weaned soul was all resign'd
   To thy most glorious will ;
Oh ! had I kept that better mind,
   Or been afflicted still !

Where are the vows which then I vow'd,
   The joys which then I knew ?
Those vanish'd like the morning cloud,
   These like the early dew.

Lord, grant me grace for every day,
   Whate'er my state may be ;
Through life, in death, with truth to say,
   " My God is all to me."

IN SORROW.

"It is thy hand, my God!
    My sorrow comes from Thee :
I bow beneath thy chastening rod—
    'Tis love that bruises me.

" I would not murmur, Lord ;
    Before Thee I am dumb,
Lest I should breathe one murmuring word ;
    To Thee for help I come.

" My God, thy name is love,
    A Father's hand is thine ;
With tearful eyes I look above,
    And cry ' Thy will be mine.'

" I know thy will is right,
    Though it may seem severe ;
Thy path is still unsullied light,
    Though dark it oft appear.

" Jesus for me hath died,
    Thy Son Thou didst not spare ;
His pierced hands, his bleeding side
    Thy love for me declare.

" Here my poor heart can rest,
    My God, it cleaves to Thee ;
Thy will is love, thine end is best,
    All work for good to me."

DECK.

AFFLICTION.

Let not the godly man affliction fear,
    God wrestle may with some, but none over-
        throws ;
Who gives the burden gives the strength to bear,
    And best reward the greatest service owes.
Those who would reap, they at the first must
        hear
    God's love, his faith a good man's trouble
        shews.
Those whom God tries, He gives them power to
        stand,
He Jacob tossed, and helped both by one hand.

William Alexander, Earl of Stirling.

LIGHT IN THE DARK VALLEY.

Aʜ! I shall soon be dying,
  Time swiftly glides away;
But on my Lord relying,
  I hail the happy day;—

The day when I shall enter
  Upon a world unknown;
My helpless soul I venture
  On Jesus Christ alone.

He once a spotless victim
  Upon Mount Calvary bled!
Jehovah did afflict Him,
  And bruise Him in my stead.

Hence all my hope arises,
  Unworthy as I am;
My soul most surely prizes
  The sin-atoning Lamb.

To Him by grace united,
 I joy in Him alone ;
And now, by faith, delighted
 Behold Him on his throne.

There He is interceding
 For all who on Him rest ;
The grace from Him proceeding
 Shall waft me to his breast.

Then, with the saints in glory,
 The grateful song I'll raise,
And chant my blissful story
 In high seraphic lays.

CONFLICT.

Oh! there are sorrows deep and hidden,
  Which He who made the heart alone can know;
When dark temptation's waves are bidden,
  The weak, the weary heart to overflow.

Crush'd to the earth, yet struggling, striving,
  To hide or overcome the war within ;
Yet left to feel the foe with strength reviving,
  The bondage harder still of grief and sin.

The captive cries—but closer, closer binding,
  His chains around him seem the more to cling ;
The weak one prays, and prays without his finding
  That prayer does his desired deliverance bring.

And can it be that Thou, the God of power,
  Hast failed?—that thy compassions cease to flow?
Wilt Thou not save me in this trying hour ?
  Thou who dost all my depth of anguish know !

Yes ; all its bitterness before Thee
　My heart hath oft-times poured forth in prayer ;
Thou, who when agony came o'er Thee,
　Didst pray—oh ! save me from despair !

Vainly to friends I look for pity,
　My soul's dark griefs they cannot feel or know ;
But, Lord, I leave my sorrows with Thee,
　For Thou alone hast power to heal my woe.

C. H. J.

DIVINE COMFORT.

O LORD ! across our path of woe,
  Some rays of heavenly comfort fling ;
Increase of love and faith bestow,
  And they their sister hope shall bring.

We wander in perplexing ways ;—
  The tempter prompts us to despair ;
In murmurings seeks to stifle praise ;
  In hopelessness to silence prayer.

It is in love, O Lord, we fail ;
  For ever, by love's glances keen,
In death, and sorrow's darkest vale,
  Thy mercies through the mist are seen.

O Lord ! we are of little faith !
  If Thou indeed hast sent from heaven
Thy son for man to suffer death,
  Hast Thou not with Him all things given ?

Teach us that wondrous love to feel ;—
 So, when a sword has pierced us through,
That thought doubt's maddening wound shall heal,
 And kindle dying hope anew.

ANSTIE.

REMEMBER ME.

O Thou, from whom all goodness flows !
    I lift my soul to Thee ;
In all my sorrows, conflicts, woes,
    Good Lord, *remember me.*

When on my aching, burdened heart,
    My sins lie heavily,
My pardon speak, new peace impart ;—
    In love *remember me.*

When trials sore obstruct my way,
    And ills I cannot flee,
Lord let my strength be as my day ;—
    For good *remember me.*

If worn with pain, disease, and grief,
    This feeble frame should be,
Grant patience, rest, and kind relief ;—
    Hear, and *remember me.*

When in the solemn hour of death,
I wait thy just decree;
Saviour, with my last parting breath
I'll cry, *remember me.*

HUMPHRIES.

VALUE OF AFFLICTIONS.

So till men's persons great afflictions touch
(If worth be found) their worth is not so much,
Because, like wheat, in straw, they have not, yet,
That value, which in threshing, they may get.
For till the bruising flailes of God's corrections,
Have threshed out of us our vaine affections;
Till those corruptions, which doe misbecome us,
Are by thy Sacred Spirit winnowed from us;
Until, from us, the straw of worldly-treasures;
Till all the dusty chaffe of empty pleasures;
Yea, till his flaile upon us he doth lay,
To thresh the huske of this our flesh away;
And leave the soule uncovered; nay, yet more,
Till God shall make our very Spirit poore;
    We shall not up to highest wealth aspire;
    But, then we shall; and that is my desire.
WITHER.

THE MOURNER'S HYMN.

THE hopes that made my gladness
  Have perished one by one,
And now in deepest sadness
  I sit and mourn alone.

My sin hath brought my sorrow,
  And Thou art righteous still :
From earth I will not borrow
  False joy, my cup to fill.

Beneath my burden sighing,
  Not one can comfort me ;
Before thine altar lying,
  My God, I wait for Thee.

In anguish I have striven
  To say—"Thy will be done ;"
Oh ! may the strength be given
  Which comes from Thee alone.

'Tis well that Thou hast taken
   Mine idol-gods away;
But why hast Thou forsaken?
   Mine everlasting stay!

When Thou hast pardon spoken
   In other times to me,
The spirit's bands were broken,
   I felt that I was free.

Would that, thy blood receiving,
   Mine heart might be at ease:
Would that, thy word believing,
   I might go forth in peace!

Then, towards thy kingdom pressing,
   Life's struggle would be brief,
And still the mourner's blessing
   Should calm the mourner's grief.

E. C. C. B.

THE DAYS OF THY MOURNING SHALL BE ENDED.

Hear what God the Lord hath spoken :
  "O, my people, faint and few ;
Comfortless, afflicted, broken,—
  Fair abodes I build for you :
Thorns of heartfelt tribulation
  Shall no more perplex your ways ;
You shall name your walls Salvation,
  And your gates shall all be Praise.

"There, like streams that feed the garden,
  Pleasures without end shall flow ;
For the Lord, your faith rewarding,
  All his bounty shall bestow :
Still, in undisturbed possession,
  Peace and righteousness shall reign ;
Never shall you feel oppression,—
  Hear the voice of war again.

"Ye, no more your suns descending,
  Waning moons, no more shall see;
But your griefs, for ever ending,
  Find eternal noon in me:
God shall rise, and shining o'er you,
  Change to day the gloom of night;
He, the Lord, shall be your glory—
  God, your everlasting light."

COWPER.

HOPE THOU IN GOD.

Thou child of God in sorrow,
  Hope for a brighter day,
The sunshine of the morrow,
  Shall chase thy griefs away.

Though racking pain distress thee
  And shake thy weary frame,
A Saviour's love shall bless thee,
  In sickness prove the same.

Thy Brother's eye beholds thee,
  His heart feels all thy woes;
His mighty arm upholds thee,
  Thine every care He knows.

Earth's rest is all polluted,
  And would thy soul destroy;
Thou'rt from this world uprooted,
  To find in Him thy joy.

Thy former friends may leave thee,
   Companions may be few,
But will not Christ receive thee,
   The faithful and the true?

Thy tried and lonely spirit
   Thirsts for the living God,
And pleads alone the merit
   Of rich redeeming blood.

Shrink not because He chastens,
   But to the end endure;
Each thrill of anguish hastens
   The hour of perfect cure.

Take up a song of gladness
   While bruised beneath the rod;
Triumphant over sadness,
   Witness before thy God.

Proclaim his sov'reign power
   O'er suffering and disease,
And in afflictions hour,
   Tell of the spirit's peace.
                        E. C. C. B.

BITTER-SWEET.

Yes; every heart its sorrow knows,
   And deep within its inmost cell,
Its cup of bitterness o'erflows;
A cup of secret, silent woes,
   Of which it may not tell.

No stranger's ear is tuned to hear;
   No stranger's heart can know or feel;
No bosom friend, however dear,
However loved, may venture near,
   Its sacred wound to heal.

But there is One who feels it all,
   Whose riven heart deep sorrow knew,
Whose bitter cup was drugged with gall;
He listens to thy whispered call,
   To every whisper true.

Each sigh makes music in his ear,
   For oh ! his heart to thine replies ;
" 'Tis I," He whispers ; " do not fear,
I come to wipe thine every tear,
   To quell thy rising sighs.

" I wept that I might know to weep,
   With all my precious, ransom'd saints ;
Their tears, their sighs, I treasured keep,
I feel their woes however deep,
   For mine are their complaints."

Then cast thy burden all on Him,
   Nor longer call thy griefs thine own ;
He turns from harps of seraphim,
To brighten up that eye so dim
   Which looks to Him alone.

C. SABINE.

SONG OF THE NEW HEAVENS AND NEW EARTH.

OH, past are the Fast Days, the Feast Day, the
    Feast Day is come,
The solitude endeth, the Guest most beloved is
    come.
Deserted one, thou hast deserted thy desert at last !
O love ! the Beloved, who cannot desert thee, is
    come ;
And sever'd the severing; departed for ever the
    parting ;
And met is the meeting : the One, the most blessed,
    is come !
The fleeting has fleeted ; the ban of the Exile is
    banish'd ;
Far distant the distance ; the Bird to the nestlings
    is come !
The Moon to the sky, to the desolate garden the Rose,
To the palace forsaken the King in his glory is come,
The Life to the root, and the Sap to the height of the
    tree :

The Wreath to the sprays, and the Crown to the
    branches, is come !
And now let him come; the assaulter who fain
    would assault me ;
I am safe in the Tower; my Tower of shelter is
    come !.
Now cast on me ever and ever the fire of love :
I fear not the fire ; my Robe of Asbestos is come !
As soon as they heard it, that Thou with salvation
    wert nigh :
Behold every heart, heavy laden with sorrow, is come !
O Vessel of Fulness, pour'd out for the thirst of the
    worlds,
We thank Thee, we thank Thee ! to us thy refreshing
    is come !
For long came no breeze to the deserts unblest ;
    and now One
With wings which the dew of all blessing has
    moisten'd, is come !
We have waited till voice of the Spring should
    awaken the dead :
Behold, from the East to the West the Spring-glory
    is come !

From the German
(*In Songs of Eternal Life*).

PEACE BE WITH YOU!

Peace be with you! saith the Lord;
Is not this a glorious word?
To the heart it brings relief,
From disquiet, pain, and grief;
Care removing instantly,
Glorious word of victory!

Glorious word of victory!
Strengthened now and cheered by thee,
While I walk the narrow way,
All my fetters fall away;
Still thou soundest full and free,
Glorious word of victory!

Glorious word of victory!
Sounding ever cheeringly,
Till all anxious storms subside,
And I hear on every side
Sound the glorious proclamation,
Perfect reconciliation.

Sacred, peaceful salutation !
Now the fruits of this salvation
Ever shall remain with me,
In time and through eternity ;
Sounding thus continually,
Glorious word of victory !

THOLUCK.

THANKFUL JOY.

Oh, there is a bed, that was hewn in stone,
Where He lay who was nailed to the tree !
'Twas there my Lord lay, all alone,
And there's the rest for me.

And there was a dew, all silvery bright,
It fell on plain and lee ;
They gather'd it fresh, at the morning light,
And sweet's its taste to me.

And there was a rushing mighty wind,
It blew o'er a *bloody sea ;*
It breathes a calm for my troubled mind,
A Comforter for me.

And there was a gale when the day-star rose ;
His shining clear I see ;
My mind, in his beams, revives and glows,
And all is life with me.

And there was a flower, which sprung from the tomb,
When the days had number'd three ;
Upon my heart that flower shall bloom,
Eternal joy for me.

BULL.

THE NIGHT SONG.

Open to Me, my sister,
  My dove, my undefiled!
Fair solitary lily
  Of all this thorny wild.
Oh, let Me see thy countenance,
  Oh, let Me hear thy voice;
For pleasant are thy tone, thy glance,
  They make my heart rejoice.

Open to Me, my sister!
  Chill is the faint moonlight;
My head is filled with dew-damp,
  My locks with drops of night.
Thou know'st not thy Beloved's voice,
  His knocking at thy door;
Strange on thine ear his pleadings fall,
  They melt thy heart no more.

Open to Me, my sister !
 Look on Me now, and see
What I have braved in battle,
 And all for love of thee.
The thorny crown my visage marr'd,
 The sharp spear pierced my side ;
The nails my hands and feet have scarr'd,
 My wounds were deep and wide.

Open to Me, my sister !
 I love, I linger yet ;
While fast the moon is waning,
 And stars begin to set.
When o'er yon hills to thee I sped,
 My step was glad and fleet ;
But sad and slow will be the tread
 Of my retiring feet,

Open to Me, my sister !
 Oh, wilt thou not invite
The world's outcast wayfarer
 To tarry for a night ?
The mountain foxes have their hole,
 The sky-birds have their nest ;
But, save in thy surrendered soul,
 I have not where to rest.   A. R. C.

CHRIST MY JOY.

Jesus, my lovinge spouse,
   Eternall veritie ;
Perfect guide of my soule,
   Way to eternitie ;
Strengthen me with thy grace,
   From Thee I'll never flee,
Let them all say what they will,
   Jesu, come Thou to me.

Poore men seeke others' wealth,
   Blinde men seeke libertie,
Crazed corpses (sick bodies) cry for health,
   All seeke prosperitie.
I nothinge seeke but Christ,
   He alone pleaseth me ;
Let them all say what they will,
   Jesu, come Thou to me.

Fervent love longeth sore
  His lady's face to see ;
Discarded courtiers seeke
  In princes' grace to be.
Noe want nor woe I feel
  Whilst I doe enjoy Thee ;
Let them all say what they will,
  Jesu, come Thou to me.

What can this wretched world,
  Repleat with miserie,
Yield to delight my soule,
  Made for eternitie.
All is vaine, all is fraile,
  All that compared to Thee ;
And earthlie things doe faile ;
  Jesu, come Thou to me.

Tho' the world tempt me sore ;
  Tho' the flesh trouble me ;
Tho' the devil would devoure ;
  My refuge is to Thee.
Tho' heaven and earthe doe faile,
  Tho' all perplexed be,
Thou art, and ever shall
  My chiefest comfort be.

Thou art my Saviour sweete,
  Foode and delight to me,
A medicine most meete
  To each infirmitie.
To my taste honey sweete,
  To my eare melodie,
Perfect guide to my feete,
  To my heart jubilee.

From an old MS. in the
British Museum.

AN .OLD EPITAPH.

HERE lies the ruined cabinet
Of a rich soul, more highly set.
The dross and refuse of a mind
Too glorious to be here confined.
Earth for a while bespoke his stay,
Only to bait, and so away;
So that what here he doated on
Was merely accommodation.
Not that his active soul could be
At home, but in eternity.
Yet while he blest us with his rays
Of his short continued days,
Each minute had its weight of worth,
Each pregnant hour some star brought forth.
So whiles he travelled here beneath,
He lived, when others only breathe.

For not a sand of time slipped by
Without its action sweet as high :
So good, so peaceable, so blest,
Angels alone can speak the rest.

CLEVELAND.

NOT MY WILL, BUT THINE BE DONE.

"FATHER! not my will, but Thine;"
   Let this be my daily prayer
Taught me by those lips divine,
   Taught me by affliction's Heir,
By "The Man of Sorrows" breathed—
He for whom earth's thorns were wreathed.

"Father! not my will, but Thine;"
   Choose for me my lot—my way;
If thy smiles around me shine,
   Sorrows night will turn to day;
Thunder-clouds be tinged with gold,
Flowers will spring, though winds be cold.

"Father! not my will, but Thine;"
   Though I lay my throbbing head
On a couch bedewed with brine,
   Tears were Jesu's daily bread;
Through the tears Thou bidst to flow
Smiles a radiant promise-bow.

"Father! not my will, but Thine;"
   Help me to believe Thee true,
Though the corn, the oil, the wine.
   Fail for lack of rain and dew:
When the springs of earth are dry,
Thou canst all my need supply.

"Father! not my will, but Thine;"
   Friends may leave me all alone;
Foes with kinsmen may combine:
   Those I love my name disown;
Still a Father Thou wilt prove;
Naught can change my Father's love.

Whatsoe'er my lot may be,
   Passing through this vale of tears,
Pain, or scorn, or penury,
   Few my yet remaining years;
Never let thy child repine,
"Father! not my will, but Thine!"

C. SABINE.

ISRAEL'S CRY.

Rock and refuge of my soul,
Swiftly let the season roll,
When thine Israel shall arise
Lovely in the nation's eyes!

Lord of glory, Lord of might,
    As our ransom'd fathers tell,
Once more for thy people fight,
    Plead for thy loved Israel.
Give our spoilers towers to be
Waste and desolate as we.

Hasten, Lord, the joyful year,
    When thy Zion, tempest-toss'd,
Shall the silver trumpet hear,
    Bring glad tidings to the lost!
Captive, cast thy cords from thee,
Loose thy neck, be free, be free.

Why dost thou behold our sadness?
 See the proud have torn away
All our years of solemn gladness,
 When thy flock kept holiday!
Lord thy fruitful vine is bare,
Not one gleaning grape is there!

Rock and refuge of my soul,
Swiftly let the season roll,
When thine Israel shall be
Once again beloved and free!
   M'CHEYNE, FROM THE HEBREW.

THE SHADOW OF THE CROSS.

O SAVIOUR, let my wearied spirit rest
   Beneath the shadow of thy cross, and send
Sweet thoughts of peace to soothe my troubled breast,
   And o'er my soul their dove-like wings extend.

Where shall I cast the burden of my life,
   The burden of my sins, if not on Thee?
My soul is grieved and wearied with the strife
   Of this rude world; receive and comfort me.

Beneath the shadow of the cross, thy child
   Shall find a refuge and a calm retreat,
Where sainted souls, with heaven reconciled,
   Await the hour when earth and heaven meet.

FROM THE " DOVE ON THE CROSS."

THE SHEPHERD AND THE REST.

O GENTLE Shepherd, guided by thy hand,
  My soul hath found her everlasting rest ;
Thou leadest me towards my Father-land,
  And on the way thy presence makes me blest !

Sadly and wearily I went along,
  Tumult and vain unrest on every hand,
Until Thou drew'st me from the noisy throng,
  And brought me to a quiet pasture-land !

And ah, what sweetness I experience there !
  The blue sky crystal clear, and from the trees
A thousand balmy odours fill the air,
  Borne on the pinions of the vernal breeze.

For heart and eye how rich the pasture spread !
  When with unceasing change by day and night,
Like a fair garb with jewels all inlaid,
  A veil of freshest flowers enchants my sight.

The noonday sun, unveiled by envious clouds,
   Calls forth their varying tints in hues of light ;
And when in evening shade his beams he shrouds,
   The violets yield their fragrance to the night.

How well the unbroken calm, so deep and still,
   My soul refreshes,—long with tumult filled ;
And now, methinks, my undivided will,
   May to my Shepherd's will for ever yield.

THOLUCK.

TRUST.

When all beneath the ample cope of heaven
I saw like clouds before the tempest driven,
In sad vicissitudes eternal round,
A while I stood in silent sadness borne,
And thus at last with self-exploring mind,
Musing, I asked, "What basis can I find
To fix my trust?"   A heavenly voice replied,
"Trust in thy God; He all thy steps shall guide,
He never fails to hear the trusting prayer;—
But worldly hope must end in dull despair."

PETRARCH.

THE BORDER-LANDS.

FATHER, into thy loving hands
   My feeble spirit I commit,
While wandering in these border-lands
   Until thy voice shall summon it.

Father, I would not dare to choose
   A longer life, an earlier death ;
I know not what my soul might lose
   By shortened or protracted breath.

These border-lands are calm and still,
   And solemn are their silent shades ;
And my heart welcomes them, until
   The light of life's long evening fades.

I heard them spoken of with dread,
   As fearful and unquiet places ;
Shades, where the living and the dead
   Look sadly in each other's faces.

But since thy hand hath led me here,
   And I have seen the border-land,
Seen the dark river flowing near,
   Stood on its brink, as now I stand;

There has been nothing to alarm
   My trembling soul; how could I fear
While thus encircled with thine arm?
   I never felt Thee half so near.

What should appal me in a place
   That brings me hourly nearer Thee?
Where I may almost see thy face—
   Surely 'tis here my soul would be.

They say the waves are dark and deep,
   That faith has perished in the river;
They speak of death with fear, and weep,
   Shall my soul perish? never, never.

I know that Thou wilt never leave
   The soul that trembles while it clings
To Thee; I know Thou wilt achieve
   Its passage on thine outspread wings.

And since I first was brought so near
  The stream that flows to the Dead Sea,
I think that it has grown more clear
  And shallow than it used to be.

I cannot see the golden gate
  Unfolding yet to welcome me ;
I cannot yet anticipate
  The joy of heaven's jubilee.

But I will calmly watch and pray,
  Until I hear my Saviour's voice
Calling my happy soul away
  To see his glory and rejoice.

FROM THE "DOVE ON THE CROSS."

APPREHENSION.

Oʜ ! save me from this hour :
    In trembling and in fear
    My flesh and heart cry out to Thee
    For it is drawing near.
Jesus, no eye but thine alone can see
My utter helplessness, my misery.

The cross is sharp, O Lord,
    And difficult to bear ;
    Yet to refuse it at thy hands,
    Thy servant would not dare.
Help me to take it up, and follow Thee
Through shame and pain, to dark Gethsemane.

There would I look on Thee,
    Thou Saviour in thy woe,
    Bleeding in agony for me,
    Bowed meekly down so low ;
There would I learn submission to thy will,
Till my rebellious heart is calm and still.

HOLY TEARS.

Yes, thou mayest weep, for Jesus shed
  Such tears as those thou sheddest now,
When, for the living or the dead,
  Sorrow lay heavy on his brow.

He sees thee weep, yet doth not blame
  The weakness of thy flesh and heart ;
Thy human nature is the same
  As that in which He took a part.

He knows its weakness, for he felt
  The crushing power of pain and woe,
How body, soul, and spirit melt
  And faint beneath the stunning blow.

What, if poor sinners count thy grief
  The sign of an unchastened will?
He who can give thy soul relief,
  Knows that thou art submissive still.

Turn thee to Him, to Him alone ;
  For all that our poor lips can say
To soothe thee, broken-hearted one,
  Would fail to comfort thee to-day.

We will not speak to thee, but sit
  In prayerful silence by thy side ;
Grief has its ebbs and flows ; 'tis fit
  Our love should wait the ebbing tide.

Jesus himself will comfort thee,
  In his own time, in his own way,
And haply more than "two or three "
  Unite in prayer for thee to-day.

FROM THE " DOVE ON THE CROSS."

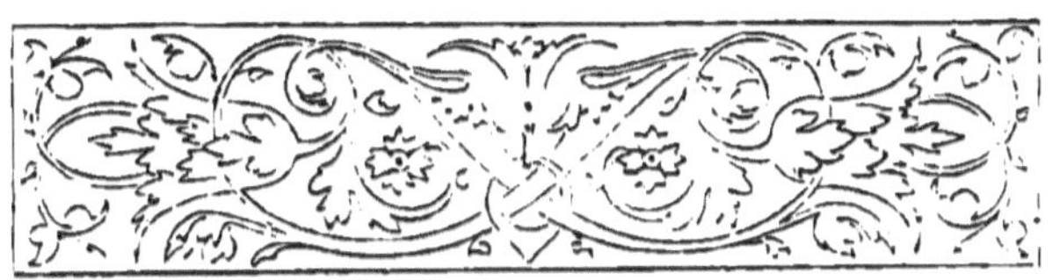

WHOM HAVE I IN HEAVEN BUT THEE.

To Thee my heart would tell its griefs, O Lord,
   My burning tears into thy bosom flow,
For thou hast promised in thy faithful Word
   That thou wilt bear the weight of all my woe.

And I am thine!   O that my life were spent
   In doing only all thy righteous will;
That I might walk, on holiness intent,
   And every hour delight to love Thee still.

Yes; I with joy from every sin would flee,
   Nor for a moment should my heart delay;
But speak the word, and that one word from Thee
   I would with willingness at once obey.

When shall the hour of my deliverance be?
   When shall the law of death no more remain?
When, my dear Saviour, shall I joyful see
   Thy love alone within my bosom reign?

Till that blest day, thy aid would I entreat,
Inspire me as the conflict I renew;
My safety is in thee—thy work complete;
O, be my Rock, and my Redeemer too!

MALAN.

THE HIDING-PLACE.

O WELCOME hiding-place !   O refuge meet
For fainting pilgrims, on this desert way !
O kind Conductor of these wandering feet,
Through snares and darkness, to the realms of day !
Soon did the Sun of Righteousness display
His healing beams ; each gloomy cloud dispel :
While on the parting mist, in colours gay,
Truth's cheering bow of precious promise fell,
And Mercy's silver voice soft whispered,—" All is
    well."

D. HUNTINGDON (AMERICAN).

RETIREMENT.

I LOVE to steal awhile away
   From every cumbering care,
And spend the hours of setting day
   In humble, grateful prayer.

I love in solitude to shed
   The penitential tear;
And all his promises to plead,
   Where none but God can hear.

I love to think on mercies past,
   And future good implore,
And all my sighs and sorrows cast
   On Him whom I adore.

I love by faith to take a view
   Of brighter scenes in heaven :
Such prospects oft my strength renew,
   While here by tempests driven.

Thus, when life's toilsome day is o'er,
    May its departing ray
Be calm as this impressive hour,
    And lead to endless day.

                ANON. (AMERICAN.)

I AM WITH YOU.

No more let sorrow cloud your eye,
   Nor fears your spirit fill ;
Though now the parting hour is nigh,
   My heart is with you still.
My Father sent me from above,
   His mercy's brightest sign,
And if you trust his changeless love,
   Oh, wherefore doubt of mine ?

The stretching shadow of the cross
   Now overcasts my soul ;
You sorrow for the coming loss,
   I long to reach the goal.
My love must first be tried by death
   Before it prove its power,
And through its triumph give you faith
   For many an evil hour.

Dark days will come when I depart,
　　But cast your care on me,
And I, unseen, will keep the heart
　　From fear and fainting free.
The thorny path that I have trod
　　Is also traced for you ;
But where I walked alone with God,
　　Ye have your Saviour too.

J. D. BURNS.

THE HEAVENLY CITY.

O`heavenly Jerusalem
  Of everlasting halls !
Thrice blessed are the people
  Thou storest in thy walls.

Thou art the golden mansion
  Where saints for ever sing ;
The seat of God's own chosen—
  The palace of the King.

There God for ever sitteth,
  Himself of all, the crown ;
The Lamb the light that shineth,
  And never goeth down.

Nought to this seat approacheth
  Their sweet peace to molest ;
They praise their God for ever,
  Nor day nor night they rest.

Calm Hope from thence is leaning,
    To her our longings bend ;
No shortlived toil shall daunt us
    For joys that cannot end.

To Christ the Son, that lightens
    His church, above, below ;
To Father and to Spirit
    All things created bow !

OLD LATIN HYMN.

PATIENCE.

THE wise man grieves not that he undergoes
Affliction, but because he fully knows
His many sins deserved as many more,
If ten times doubl'd, than he did before.
    Patience in things adverse, like stars, shine
        bright
    And most transparent in the darkest night.

JOHN QUARLES.

AS THOU WILT.

THIS then must be the med'cine for my woes,
To yield to what my Saviour shall dispose ;
To glory in my baseness ; to rejoice
In mine afflictions ; to obey his voice,
As well when threatenings my defects reprove,
As when I cherished am with words of love ;
To say to Him in every time and place—
Withdraw thy comforts, so Thou leave thy grace.

BEAUMONT.

SONG OF THE ETERNAL SABBATH.

THERE is a day of rest before thee—
Thou weary soul, arise and shine !
Awhile the clouds hang darkly o'er thee,
Awhile the captive's chains are thine.
    Behold the Lamb of God will lead thee
    To still green pastures round the throne.
    Cast off thy burden, rise and speed thee,
    For soon the battle storm is done,—
For soon the weary race is past,
And thou shalt rest in love at last.

God stablished ere the days of heaven
Rest, gentle rest, for evermore ;
Men long have wept, and toiled and striven,
But rest was ordered long before.
    For this the Saviour left the skies,
    The home beyond the thousand suns ;—
    He stretches forth his hands, and cries,
    " Come, come to me ye weary ones !

Ye long have laboured, come and rest,
Lie still, beloved, on my breast."

Then come ye sorrowful and weary,
Ye heavy-laden come to Him,
From desert places, lone and dreary,
With fainting heart and aching limb !
   For ye have borne the heat of day,
   And now the hour of rest is come ;
   To you the Lord doth call and say—
   " My people I will be your home !
Fear not for devil, world, and sin,
But saved and pardoned enter in."

Come in, the sheaves of glory bringing,
The seed-time of our tears is past ;
More sweet than dreams of joy the singing
That fills our Father's house at last :
   And grief, and fear, and death, and pain,
   Are fled, and are forgotten things :
   We see the Lamb that once was slain,—
   He leads us to the living springs ;
Himself he wipes our tears away—
Such blessedness no words can say.

The day of deep refreshing dawneth,
No sun lights on us, and no heat ;
No longer is there one who mourneth,
And there the long, long severed meet,
 And God Himself shall be with them.
 They who the weary desert trod
 Shall be a royal diadem
 For ever in the hand of God ;
All hail ! thou glorious Sabbath-day,
When toil and strife are passed away !

And peace is round us as a river,
And glory as a flowing stream ;
With Christ our Lord we dwell for ever,
For ever lean in love on Him.
 Oh, had we wings to flee away,
 Afar into that holy home !
 Why seek we still on earth to stay ?
 The Spirit and the Bride say, " Come."
Arise !   Salvation draweth near,
The everlasting Sabbath year !
    JOHANNES SIEGMUND KUNTH
     (*From Songs of Eternal Life*).

SONG OF RESIGNATION.

Thou sweet beloved Will of God,
My anchor-ground, my fortress-hill,
The spirit's silent fair abode,
In thee I hide me and am still.

O Will, that willest good alone,
Lead thou the way, thou guidest best;
A silent child, I follow on,
And trusting lean upon thy breast.

God's will doth make the bitter sweet,
And all is good when it is done;
Unless God's will doth hallow it,
The glory of all joy is gone.

When Sin and World and Devil rave,
I think "God wills that it should be,
And He will strengthen, He will save:"
So trust Him calmly, joyfully.

Self, sense, and reason, they may scorn
   That hidden way that leads on high,—
Still be my deepest will uptorn,
   And so the will of nature die.

And if in gloom I see thee not,
   I lean upon thy love unknown ;—
In me thy blessed will is wrought,
   If I will nothing of my own.

O spirit of a little child,
   Of will bereft, all angel-pure,
I seek thy glory undefiled ;
   Lord, take my will, thy love is sure.

O Will of God, my soul's desire,
   My bread of life in want and pain :
O Will of God, my guiding fire,
   Unite my will to thine again.

O Will, in me thy work be done,
   For time and for eternity ;
Give joy or sorrow, all is one,
   To the blest soul that loveth Thee.

Lord, help me, kill this will of mine—
The evil power that lingers still ;
That I may be for ever thine,
And live for ever to thy will.

Tersteegen.

(*Translated in Songs of Eternal Life.*)

EVENING SONG.

THE day is gone—my soul looks on,
  To that Eternal Day,
When our sorrow and our sin
  Shall all have passed away.

The night is here—O be thou near,
  Lord Jesus, with thy light,
That my sin may flee away
  Like shadows of the night.

The golden sun is sunk and gone,
  Thou light of heaven above,
Shine through clouds and darkness down,
  And light me with thy love.

Each living thing lies slumbering,
  From care and labour free ;
May I, Lord, be still, and watch
  Thy hidden work in me.

But when shall cease the changefulness
  Of morning and of night?
When the glory of the Lord
  Shall be the living light.

No cloud shall come, no evening gloom
  On Salem shall descend;
The Lord her everlasting light,—
  Her mourning at an end.

All praise to Thee, O there to be,
  Amidst that music flood!
The many waters echoing round
  The golden shores of God.

O Jesus mine, Thou rest divine,
  Lead me to Zion's height,
That I, with all thy ransomed ones.
  May walk with Thee in white.

FREYLINGHAUSEN.

(Translated in Songs of Eternal Life.)

I WILL NOT LEAVE YOU.

Now the hour is drawing near
    Which your Master shall remove ;
Little children do not fear,
    He shall not forego his love ;
With the banner'd cross unfurl'd
Fear no tumults of the world.

When He wills, the parting storm
    Shall an azure sky disclose ;
Thence shall stoop joy's deathless form
    Smiling on your vanished woes ;
While the world's brief pleasures flow
To the sea of endless woe.

He who as a brother died,
    And in the cold grave below
Laid Him by his brethren's side,
    He shall hence before you go,
And take you with Him to dwell
In glory unapproachable.

May we here, Lord, die with Thee,
  And with thy true wisdom wise,
Put on immortality,
  Having treasure in the skies,
Where all things with one accord
Sing the Triune Holy Lord.

FROM THE LATIN.

DESIRE OF DEATH.

WHEN strongest my desire of death,
    I least am fit to die;
Because the will which keeps my breath,
    I then would fain deny.

Why would the servant, ere the time,
    Enter the Master's room,
Who may, as for a heedless crime,
    To longer waiting doom?

The angel who would change his place,
    For work or watch ordained,
God might well exile from his face,
    As one with folly stained.

'Tis the same course, the saint above,
    And earthly fellow suits;
To serve and sing, to look and love,
    And bring the Lord his fruits.

I must, by longer stay on earth,
    Better for heaven prepare :
I may not go, with such a dearth
    Of graces needful there.

God, more of strength for duty give ;
    More patience, Christ, supply ;
When longer I am fit to live,
    I shall be fit to die.

LORD KINLOCH.

TRIUMPH OVER DEATH.

Yes, thou shalt rise again, my dust, more blest
After thy hasty rest.
Undying life to live,
Will He who made thee give.
    Praised be He !

Sown but to bloom again once more, was I.
The harvest Lord goes by ;
He gathers in the sheaves,
Nor thine, nor mine, He leaves.
    Praised be He !

Oh, day of gratitude ! Oh, day of bliss !
God's own best day is this,
Which, my short slumber o'er,
From the cold grave once more
    Shall wake me.

How like a dream will it then seem to me !
With Jesus shall I be ;
In all his joys I share,
Each weary pilgrim care
　　Is past for me.

Oh ! to the Holiest, my Redeemer, lead ;
Then shall I live indeed
In sanctity, there raise
My voice, his name to praise,
　　For evermore !
FROM THE GERMAN.

THE CONSOLATION OF THE BEREAVED.

LIFE's load is heavy, and we bow
   Beneath the burden wearily ;
But shall we faint in weakness, now
      That *one* is free ?

Life's way is dark, the clouds of woe
   Veil the faint star-beams from our sight ;
Yet press we onward, for we know
      One is in light !

Life's course is long, our weary hearts
   Pant for the goal with toil distrest ;
Yet strength the blessed thought imparts,
      One is at rest !

Life's pains are sharp ; the aching head
   Seeks a short hour of rest in vain ;
Yet on *one* brow repose is shed—
      One has no pain !

Life's dreary waste is wild and rude,
    And shelterless our footsteps roam;
Yet is our failing strength renew'd—
        One is at home!

Life's wants are fierce: from burning thirst
    No stream our spirits may restore;
One dwells where living fountains burst,
        And thirsts no more!

Life's conflict thickens: from the strife,
    Wounded and worn, we seek release;
But the rude warfare still is rife—
        One is in peace!

Life's ills are piercing! wild the woe
    Fills the lone heart by grief opprest;
Yet 'midst our tears 'tis bliss to know
        That *one* is blest!

CAROLINE DENT.

BEARING THE CROSS.

THE heavier cross, the nearer heaven :
    No cross without, no God within ;
Death, judgment, from the heart are driven,
    Amidst the world's false glare and din.
      O happy he, with all his loss,
      Whom God hath set beneath the cross !

The heavier cross, the better Christian ;
    This is the touchstone God applies.
How many a garden would lie wasting,
    Unwet by showers from weeping eyes !
      The gold by fire is purified ;
      The Christian is by trouble tried.

The heavier cross, the stronger faith ;
    The loaded palm strikes deeper root ;
The vine juice sweetly issueth
    When men have pressed the clustered fruit :
      And courage grows where dangers come,
      Like pearls beneath the salt sea foam.

The heavier cross, the heartier prayer;
  The bruised herbs most fragrant are;
If wind and sky were always fair,
  The sailor would not watch the star;
    And David's Psalms had ne'er been sung;
    If grief his heart had never wrung.

The heavier cross, the more aspiring;
  From vales we climb to mountain crest;
The pilgrim, of the desert tiring,
  Longs for the Canaan of his rest.
    The dove has here no rest in sight,
    And to the ark she wings her flight.

The heavier cross, the easier dying;
  Death is a friendlier face to see;
To life's decay one bids defying;
  From life's distress one then is free.
    The cross sublimely lifts our faith
    To Him who triumphed over death.

Thou crucified! the cross I carry;
  The longer may it dearer be;
And, lest I faint whilst here I tarry,
  Implant Thou such an heart in me,
    That faith, hope, love, may flourish there,
    Till, for my cross, the crown I wear.

ANON.

JERUSALEM AND THE MORNING STAR.

THE morning star is beaming ;
Its gentle lustre streaming
　　Full in the sleeper's face.
And yet the sleeper dreameth,
And wearily she seemeth
　　Her bygone woes to trace.

She sorely comfort needeth ;
And yet no comfort heedeth ;
　　Afflicted and forlorn.
Her inmost heart is grieved ;
Of all her sons bereaved ;
　　She can but weep and mourn.

Her midnight lamp hath failed ;
And deepest gloom prevailed
　　Around yon widowed queen.
Yet still sweet hope abideth ;
And while despair derideth,
　　The morning star is seen !

The morning star is beaming ;
Its gentle lustre streaming
　　Full in the sleeper's face.
And yet the sleeper dreameth ;
And wearily she seemeth,
　　Her bygone woes to trace.

Long ages hath she slumbered.
Her hours of grief are numbered ;
　　For many seek her peace.
The eastern sky is lighter,
The mountain tops grow brighter,
　　Soon shall her sorrows cease.

The grateful dew is falling.
The early watchmen calling,
　　"Zion arise and shine;
The words of comfort greet thee,
Thy Bridegroom comes to meet thee,
　　Rise, Israel, rise and shine."

Mrs. Finn.

OUR EARTHLY SOJOURN.

I LOOK abroad upon the verdant fields,
  The song of birds is on the summer air ;
Within, how many a treasure sometimes yields,
  To bless my life, and round the edge of care ;
      And yet the earth and air,
      All that seems good and fair,
    That still is mine, or once hath been,
  Now teach me, I am but a pilgrim here,
    Without a home, and dwelling in an inn.

Not ever has the outlook been so clear :
  There have been days when stormy gusts went by ;
Nights when my wearied heart was full of fear,
  And God seemed further off than stars and sky ;
      Yet then when grief was nigh,
      My soul could sometimes cry
    Out of the depths of sorrow and of sin,
  That at the worst, I was but a pilgrim here,
    With home beyond, while dwelling in an inn.

Now I complain not of this life of mine,
  I less of shade have had than of the sun;
The gracious Father, with a hand divine,
  Has crowned with mercies his unworthy one;
    My cup has overrun,
    And I, his will undone,
  Have changed his blessings into sin,
  As I forgot I was but a pilgrim here,
    Homeless at best, and dwelling as in an inn.

Look at me, Lord! Have I not need to pray
  That this fair world, which gives so much to me,
Serve not to lead my steps so far astray
  That at the end they leave me not with Thee?
    Dear Lord, let not this be;
    Nay, rather let me see
  Beyond this life my days begin,
  And singing on my way, a pilgrim here,
    Rejoice that I am dwelling in an inn.

Dear Son of God! by whom this world was made,
  Yet homeless had not where to lay thy head;
(Not e'en by kindred was thy body laid
  In Joseph's tomb—thou Lord of quick and dead!)
    By thy example led,

Of me may it be said,
When I shall rest and peace begin,
He lived as one who was a pilgrim here,
And found his home while dwelling in an inn.

D. F. RANDOLPH.

A HYMN.

Jesus! the ladder of my faith
  Rests on the jasper walls of heaven ;
And through the veiling clouds I catch
  Faint visions of the mystic Seven.

The glory of the rainbowed throne
  Illumes those clouds like lambent flame ;
As once, on earth, thy love divine
  Burned through the robe of human shame.

Thou art the same, O gracious Lord !
  The same dear Christ that Thou wert then ;
And all the praises angels sing
  Delight Thee less than prayers of men.

We have no tears Thou wilt not dry ;
  We have no wounds Thou wilt not heal ;
No sorrows pierce our human hearts,
  That Thou, dear Saviour, dost not feel,

Thy pity, like the dew, distils ;
 And thy compassion, like the light,
Our every morning overfills,
 And crowns with stars our every night.

Let not the world's rude conflict drown
 The charmed music of thy voice,
That calls all weary souls to rest,
 And bids all mourning souls rejoice.

ANON.

I MOVE INTO THE LIGHT.

Out of the shadows that shroud the soul,
Out of the seas where the sad waves roll,
Far from the whirl of each mundane pole,
        "I move into the light!"

Out of the region of cloud and rain,
Out of the cares that oppress the brain,
Out of the body of sin and pain,
        "I move into the light!"

Out of the struggles of church and state,
Out of the empire of pride and hate,
Up through the beautiful sapphire gate,
        "I move into the light!"

Beyond the noise of creation's jars,
Higher than all the worlds and stars,
Higher than limits of reason's bars,
        "I move into the light!"

We follow after to those high spheres ;
Notes of thy rapture fall on our ears ;
Out of our darkness, our sins, and fears,
   " *We* move into the light !"

       ANON.

DYING IN THE LORD.

How blest the righteous when he dies !
  When sinks a weary soul to rest,
How mildly beam the closing eyes ;
  How gently heaves the expiring breast !

So fades a summer cloud away ;
  So sinks the gale when storms are o'er ;
So gently shuts the eye of day ;
  So dies a wave along the shore.

A holy quiet reigns around,
  A calm which life nor death destroys ;
Nothing disturbs that peace profound
  Which his unfetter'd soul enjoys.

Farewell, conflicting hopes and fears,
  Where lights and shades alternate dwell !
How bright the unchanging morn appears ;
  Farewell, inconstant world, farewell !

BARBAULD.

MY LIFE'S A SHADE.

My life's a shade, my days
    Apace to death decline;
My Lord is life, he'll raise
    My flesh again, even mine.
      Sweet truth to me,
        I shall arise,
          And with these eyes
      My Saviour see.

My peaceful grave shall keep
    My bones till that sweet day
I wake from my long sleep,
    And leave my bed of clay.
      Sweet truth to me, etc.

My Lord his angels shall
    Their golden trumpets sound,
At whose most welcome call
    My grave shall be unbound.
      Sweet truth to me, etc.

What means my beating heart
  To be afraid of death ?
My life and I shan't part,
  Tho' I resign my breath.
    Sweet truth to me, etc.

I said sometimes with tears,
  Ah, me ! I'm loath to die ;
Lord, silence thou these fears,
  My life's with Thee on high.
    Sweet truth to me, etc.

Then welcome harmless grave,
  By thee to Heaven I'll go ;
My Lord his death shall save
  Me from the flames below.
    Sweet truth to me, etc.

CROSSMAN.

ONWARD.

RISE, my soul, thy God directs thee,
  Stranger hands no more impede ;
Pass thou on, his strength protects thee,
  Strength that has the captive freed.

Is the wilderness before thee—
  Desert lands where drought abides ?
Heavenly springs shall there restore thee,
  Fresh from God's exhaustless tides.

Light divine surrounds thy going,
  God himself shall mark thy way ;
Secret blessings, richly flowing,
  Lead to everlasting day.

God, thine everlasting portion,
  Feeds thee with the mighty's meat ;
Sav'd from Egypt's hard extortion,
  Egypt's food no more to eat.

Art thou wean'd from Egypt's pleasures ?
   God, in secret, shall thee keep ;
There unfold his hidden treasures,—
   There his love's exhaustless deep.

In the desert God will teach thee
   What the God that thou hast found,—
Patient, gracious, powerful, holy ;—
   All his grace shall there abound.

On to Canaan's rest still wending,
   E'en thy wants and woes shall bring
Suited grace from high descending,—
   Thou shalt taste of mercy's spring.

Though thy way be long and dreary,
   Eagle strength He'll still renew ;
Garments fresh, and feet unweary,
   Tell how God hath brought thee through.

When to Canaan's long-loved dwelling
   Love divine thy foot shall bring,
There, with shouts of triumph swelling,
   Zion's songs in rest to sing.

There no stranger-God shall meet thee ;—
Stranger thou in courts above !
He who to his rest shall greet thee,
Greets thee with a well-known love.

       DARBY.

HOPE IN LONELINESS.

OH, what a lonely path were ours,
   Could we, O Father, see,
No home of rest beyond it all,
   No guide or help in Thee.

But Thou art near, and with us still,
   To keep us on the way
That leads along this vale of tears
   To the bright world of day.

There shall thy glory, O our God !
   Break fully on our view :
And we, thy saints, rejoice to find
   That all thy word was true.

There Jesus, on his heavenly throne,
   Our wond'ring eyes shall see :
While we, the blest associates there
   Of all his joy shall be.

Sweet hope ! we leave without a sigh
 A blighted world like this ;
To bear the cross, despise the shame,
 For all that weight of bliss.

Yet little do thy saints, at best,
 Endure, O Lord, for Thee,
Whose suffering soul bore all our sins
 And sorrows on the tree :

Who faced our fierce and ruthless foe,
 Unaided and alone ;
To win us for thy crown of joy,
 To raise us to thy throne.

Sir E. Denny.

EXTRA PORTAM.

The following is a translation of the Latin hymn of Hildebert, written about the close of the eleventh century. The reader will recognise four great Bible scenes in it—first, the raising of the widow's son ; second, the stilling of the storm ; third, the barren fig tree ; fourth, the casting out of the evil spirit from the child. It is only part of a larger poem, the terse Latinity and metaphysical Augustinianism of which make the translation a work of great difficulty.

From the gate now carried forth,
Putrid, covered, earth with earth ;
Bound, the stone upon him lies,
If thou biddest, he shall rise.
Speak the word, back rolls the stone ;
Speak the word, the shroud is gone ;
All on wing, he hastes to come,
When Thou sayest leave the tomb.

On this ocean's troubled breast
Pirate bands my bark infest;
Here the foe and there the wave,
Death and trouble round me rave.
Come, good Helmsman, come at last,
Smooth the sea and hush the blast,
Bid these pirates turn and flee,
Bring to port my bark and me.

Barren fig-tree sure am I
Every branch is bare and dry.
Hew and burn—it merits all—
Justly would the sentence fall.
Yet one other year, oh spare,
Dig it, dung it, it may bear;
If not, then the fire, ah me,
Must consume the fruitless tree.

'Gainst me the old enemy
Flood and flame doth fiercely ply;
Faint, afflicted, there is none
Left for me but Thou alone.
That this enemy may flee,
That the sick one healed may be,
Help thy sick one night and day,
Help him, Lord, to fast and pray;—

This the Lord would have us know ;
Shall deliver from this foe.
From his grasp my soul unwind ;
Give the loyal lowly mind ;
Give, oh give, the fear divine,
Lacking which no heaven is mine ;
Give hope, faith, and charity,
Give me prudent piety ;
Give contempt of earthly toys,
Appetite for heavenly joys.

Thou art all of hope to me ;
All, O God, I seek from Thee.
Thee my praise, my good I call ;
Thou my gift, and Thou my all.
Thou in toil my solace art,
Cordial of my fainting heart.
Thou in grief my lyre, O God ;
Thou the lightener of the rod.
Thou in bonds me settest free,
Thou in falls upliftest me !
Still in wealth bestowing fear,
Still in want preserving cheer.
Injured, Thou requitest ill,
Threatened, Thou defendest still :

What is dark Thou dost unseal,
What needs veiling Thou dost veil.

Ah, Thou wilt not let me go,
To the prison-cells below,
Where the sorrow, where the fear,
Where the stench, and where the tear;
Where all sin is brought to light,
And the guilty plunged in night.
Where the torturer ceaseth never,
Where the worm shall gnaw for ever:
Endless all, unchangeable;
Endless death, and endless hell.

Mine be Zion, city blest,
Zion, David's seat of rest;
She whose Former formed the light,
She whose gate the cross makes bright,
She whose keys are Peter's voice,
She whose dwellers all rejoice;
Living stones her walls do fill,
King of joy her guardian still;
Here is light without decay,
Spring eternal peace for aye.
Fragrance filling heaven on high,
Ever festal melody.

No corruption taints its air,
No defect, no murmur there,
None there dwarfed and none deformed,
All to Christ have been conformed.

Heavenly city, city blest,
On the rock securely placed,
In thy haven calmly set,
From afar thy walls I greet ;
Thee I hail, for thee I sigh,
Thee I love, for thee I cry.
How thy sons rejoice in love,
How they keep the feast above,
What they feel mid yonder light,
Or what gems their walls make bright,
Jacinth's or chalcedon's glow,—
They who are within thee know !—

In the streets of yonder city,
　May I, with the holy throng,
Joined with Moses and Elias,
　Sing the Hallelujah song.

INDEX TO FIRST LINES.

www.ingramcontent.com/pod-product-compliance
Lightning Source LLC
Chambersburg PA
CBHW031153120726
47905CB00006B/1926